Memory
for
Management

by

Paul A. Douglas

BELFAST BOOKS

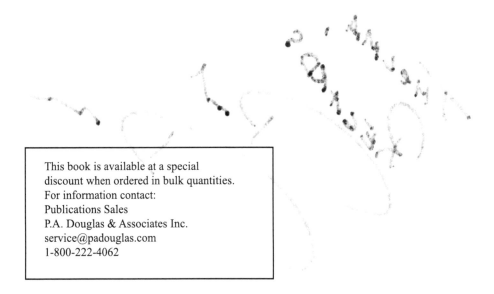

This book is available at a special
discount when ordered in bulk quantities.
For information contact:
Publications Sales
P.A. Douglas & Associates Inc.
service@padouglas.com
1-800-222-4062

Library of Congress Control Number: 2010906707

Douglas, Paul A.

   Memory for Management / Paul A. Douglas
   p. cm.
   Includes index
   ISBN 978-0-919917-10-1
   1. Memory Improvement   2. Management   3. Psychology, industrial

I. Douglas, Paul A.

II. Title
BF385

This publication is produced to provide current authoritative information on the subject matter covered. It is sold with the express understanding that the author and/or publisher is not engaging in rendering psychological, legal, or other professional services. If legal, psychological, or other expert assistance is required, a competent professional should be sought.

Printing number
10 9 8 7 6 5 4 3 2

MEMORY FOR MANAGEMENT
Lighting Your Way To Excellence

To My Five Children

I dedicate this book to my five incredible children, Thomas, Patrick, Elyse, James and Kelley. The memories I have of them are priceless.

Contents

Chapter 7

Chapter 8

Preface

To master your memory is to invite success in business, in education and in your relationships. A good memory is an absolute necessity in today's competitive work environment. In your professional life, as well as in your social life, the ability to remember names and faces, speak publicly without the need for written notes and recall dates, appointments, numbers and other important data is of immeasurable importance.

The executive, manager or administrative professional with a trained memory will see a vast improvement in his or her business life. Confidence will increase as will productivity.

Memory improvement is an essential topic in management development. Yet, in the past it was largely entertainers who taught these important business skills. Their emphasis being on delivering amazing demonstrations of memory prowess or providing tricks for remembering playing cards, rather than offering useful tools for improving an individual's business or professional skills.

In this book I will provide you with a practical course in memory improvement designed specifically to serve the needs of managers, executives and professionals. The techniques and skills presented are based on nearly forty years of research working with tens of thousands of executives, managers and professionals.

In this practical, no-nonsense book I will teach you how to speak publicly or conduct interviews without notes. I will teach you how to learn and recall the names and faces of customers, clients and others as well as important facts and details about them. I will also show you how to remember appointments and important corporate dates as well as numeric data, lists and sequential information.

Many business people believe that individuals with remarkable memories were born with that gift that, like IQ, memory abilities are set by genetics and are largely unchangeable.

I can tell you that the vast majority of individuals who can impress others with their gift of memory have developed the mnemonic skills that you will discover in this book.

It's not how "smart" you are that determines your success in remembering. It is the habits you develop and systems you use. You do not have to be a genius to remember everything you need to know; indeed the research clearly shows that the relationship between intelligence and memory is tenuous at best. The plain truth is that almost everyone can see a remarkable improvement in their ability to remember by the development and application of a few simple mnemonic skills.

If you would like to develop a great memory, a memory so powerful that you never again forget a name, appointment, speech, or idea, then you have come to the right place.

Memory For Management will help you develop the greatest "time-management" tool of all - a powerful memory.

Paul A. Douglas
March 2011

Introduction

Much of your daily life revolves around memory.

If you lost your memory, what would your life be like? If all you had was your autonomic responses such as breathing and your instinctual responses such as eating and sex, what would your day be like?

You really wouldn't know what to wear or even what to have for breakfast let alone how to prepare it. You could not remember what time to leave for work or even how a clock works. This, of course, this wouldn't matter since you had also forgotten what your job is as well as all the skills required to accomplished it.

You would have to be driven everywhere because, of course, you had forgotten how to drive a car, a good thing since you had also forgotten the rules of the road. Does red mean stop or go?

Think of the frustration you would feel, particularly in view of the fact that you could not express it having also forgotten all the skills and complexities of language.

Clearly you could not function, even survive, without your memory.

In a more somber note, for those of us who have seen the essence of a loved one slowly disappear through the ravages of Alzheimer's disease, no one has to tell us how important memory is to who we are.

Recall is *essential* to every aspect of your being.

If losing your memory would greatly diminish your effectiveness and negatively impact on every aspect of your life, then the corollary is that improving your memory will greatly increase your effectiveness and positively impact on every aspect of your life, not just as a manager but as a fully functioning multifaceted human being.

To master your memory is to invite success in your business and professional life and perhaps more importantly the relationships you have with other people.

Early in his presidency, Barack Obama came under fire for what some claimed was the overuse of a teleprompter.

The president's reliance on the innocuous machine came to light as a result of a number of "equipment malfunctions" like the time when introducing the Irish prime minister and he introduced himself. It would seem that the president wouldn't go anywhere without his teleprompter.

Observation became criticism when it was reported that he used a podium and teleprompter to address a sixth grade classroom.

This of course became fodder for the Fox News pundits, late night comedians and the writers at Saturday Night Live and resulted in Obama being referred to, at least in some circles, as the "teleprompter president."

Obama's reliance on the teleprompter seems particularly strange insofar as he is a skilled orator.

In commenting on Obama's reliance on the teleprompter, Ari Fleischer, former spokesman for George W. Bush, said, "It removes you from the audience in the room, when speaking from notes, the president can raise his head and make eye contact with the audience, as opposed to focusing on the teleprompter to his left and right." Bush, Fleischer added, "would use the teleprompter for his major big events, but when he would travel around the country, he would almost always work off large index cards."

Recognizing that Fleischer is clearly partisan and continues to function as Bush's apologist, I agree with Fleischer's assessment.

There is a place for the teleprompter, and if used judiciously it can be a very useful tool. I would suggest, however that both Bush and Obama would come across much more impressively if they could speak without *either* the teleprompter or the "large index cards."

Would be presidential candidate Sarah Palin was also derided when she made use of what some people referred to as the "Hillbilly Palm Pilot" referring to notes she had written on her palm when delivering a speech.

Ironically, she made the mistake of waving her hands around as she criticized President Obama for his use of a teleprompter.

Why the use of these strategies? Because, like most other people, neither Obama, Bush nor Palin had developed the skills that would make these devices or "cheats" unnecessary.

Executives, managers, and professionals are increasingly being asked to deliver speeches, give presentations and conduct interviews. Often on short notice. To be able to prepare for these activities in an efficient manner and deliver with confidence is an essential skill and just one example of where a good memory or, more accurately, a trained memory, can make a real difference.

In your role as manager or supervisor, have you ever come out of an interview and said to yourself, "I should have said this," or "I should have said that first," or "I shouldn't have said that at all!" the systems we will introduce you to in this chapter will help.

If you are a sales professional, your ability to memorize your sales story as well as myriad product codes, applications and other information is vital to your success as is the ability to recall vital information about your clients and prospects as well as their families.

If you are an administrative professional, the practical uses of a trained memory are vast and numerous. You are the gatekeeper. As your boss's representative, you are often the first contact people have with your manager and your office.

There are few positions where it is so vitally important to remember names and faces. The ability to remember, not only their name and organization, but also family details, interests, etc., is the sign of a truly professional administrative or executive assistant.

The impact of downsizing and organizational reengineering has extended to the executive suite. Research has shown that the average executive is working longer hours than they did a decade ago.

As a result, like many of us, the executive has fallen victim to information overload. To these busy pressured senior managers, the value of an administrative professional who ensures that nothing falls between the cracks is absolutely invaluable.

If you are an administrative professional, do you work for a boss who runs through the office saying, "don't forget to do this," or " make sure and pick such and such up," or "remind me to call so and so." How valuable would it be to have the ability to instantly lock those things into your memory and not have to be constantly scribbling things down?

In short, whether you are a manager, executive, salesperson or administrative professional, a trained memory will give you an edge, and in today's competitive work environment that edge can make a difference. A great memory is an impressive thing. You will be noticed, and your confidence will increase.

A fad is defined as, ""fashion that is taken up with great enthusiasm for a brief period of time." There have been many fads in business training. MBO, One Minute Management, Quality Circles, TQM and Japanese Management, The Seven Habits, and Six Sigma just to mention a few. Each of these programs had their value but in many ways they presented old wine in new bottles.

We have been teaching interpersonal skills in management for more than sixty years but when you cut to the bone, the common message in all these programs is this; take an interest in your employees, involve them in decision-making, treat them as if they are your most valued resource because they are.

The craving for recognition and appreciation is one of the deepest human emotions. Everyone wants to feel valued and important.

What message does it send to your staff when you cannot remember their name? Does your employee feel important when you can't remember their wife's name or their children's names, or even if they are married or have children?

I honestly believe that teaching managers how to remember names is perhaps the greatest interpersonal skills we can teach.

I've seen what it does when the president of a large corporation greets a foreman on the shop floor by name and asks his employee how his wife Alice is doing, or whether Bobbie is still on the varsity team.

I've seen how a street cop feels when the chief of police calls him by his first name.

I've have witnessed how the tone of a tough interviewer changes when the political leader of a nation calls her by name.

Many of our most revered political leaders had the ability to make others feel good about themselves.

There is a story about a person meeting President Kennedy at a rally years ago. As the President worked his way down the rope line, he shook hands and introduced himself to everyone along the way. This man shook the President's hand and introduced himself.

On his way out, the President's eye caught the man's eye to which the President said "Very nice to meet you, Jeff."

Bill Clinton utilized his memory to the amazement of others. David Gallen in his book, Bill Clinton, As They Know Him talks about when he interviewed several dozen Arkansas journalists, politicians, friends and associates of Bill, they all talked their heads off about his amazing memory for the faces, names, family members, and illnesses of what seems to be half of Arkansas.

Ronald Reagan talks about how he learned early in his life the importance of memory.

In 2010 however, Ron Reagan, the son of the 40th president wrote a book in which he suggested that his father suffered from Alzheimer's disease during his presidency.

This speculation ignited a very strong response from many quarters, particularly from his brother, Mike Reagan, who called Ron an "embarrassment" to their family.

In discounting Ron's assessment, Dr. Paul Kengo one of Reagan's biographers in his book, *The Truth About Ronald Reagan's Mind - and Memory* tells the story of a March 1986 exchange between Reagan and then Secretary of Education Bill Bennett regarding an education report.

Knowing that Reagan's memory was exceptional and his 75-year-old brain sharp, Bennett confidently put Reagan on the spot in front of a group of educators at the White House. Bennett asked the president if he recalled a verse from a Robert Service poem.

Here's a direct transcript from the official Presidential Papers:

Secretary Bennett: Mr. President, I was telling the audience before you came that memorization figures in this book fairly prominently, and I am told that you're the world champion memorizer. Do you recall something that starts "There are strange things done in the midnight sun ... ?"

The President: "... by the men who moil for gold." [Laughter]

Secretary Bennett: "The Arctic trails have their secret tales ..."

The President: "... that would make your blood run cold." [Laughter]

Secretary Bennett: I give up. I give up. I give up. Do you want to finish, Mr. President?

The President: I don't know whether in school they still read Robert W. Service but to just conclude that particular stanza, it would then be: "There are strange things-" No, we've done that. All right.

Secretary Bennett: "The North Lights have seen ..."

The President: "The Northern Lights have seen queer sights, but the queerest they ever did see was that night in the marge of Lake Lebarge I cremated Sam McGee."

There are many stories about Napoleon Bonaparte's outstanding memory. It was reported that Napoleon memorized the rosters of all his units. Then when reviewing the troops, he would greet each soldier by name, causing them to feel a personal connection to their French emperor.

Being a boss is not an easy job. Being a leader is even more difficult. As a manager or executive you have the privilege and the responsibility of managing others. But if you do not want your employees to constantly talk behind your back or complain about you, then you should cultivate the qualities of a true professional. One of the most important of those qualities is taking the time to learn the names of your people and also taking the time to develop the simple techniques we will present here for remembering them.

Memory Myths and Mechanisms

You have no doubt heard others say, and perhaps have said yourself, such things as "My memory failed me," or "I have a bad memory." These statements would suggest that "memory" exists in an almost physical sense.

We use these expressions in the same manner as, "My heart failed me," or "I have a bad leg."

The simple truth is that the object "memory" does not exist in a physical sense. Recent studies have indicated that contrary to the widely held view memory itself cannot be found in one location within the brain.

Memory is still not very well understood and something of an abstraction. It might best be thought of as a set of abilities, skills and characteristics rather than a location, an object or thing.

The misconception that memory is an object perhaps stems from the "classic education" concept born in Great Britain in the 19th century, and which still greatly influences today's education.

It was believed that the mind, very much like a muscle, could be trained and strengthened by exercise. This concept, known as a "doctrine of formal discipline" was at the root of the obsession with the teaching of rather rigorous, if not irrelevant, subjects such as Latin and Greek in school.

It was held that the mind (and the memory) was exercised and strengthened by having the student tackle and master such challenging subjects.

It was further held that this strengthened mind could then solve complex problems better and deal more effectively with other subjects and learning situations.

The research, however, does not support this view.

In an important paper published in 1924, E.L. Thorndike discounted the value of prior study to current assignments as did the outstanding American psychologist William James.

James tested whether the memory could be improved through practice by memorizing 158 lines of Victor Hugo's works.

Keeping careful notes, he found it took him an average of 60 seconds to memorize a line James then spent the next 38 days memorizing the poems of Milton.

At the conclusion of these 38 days of practice and memorization he again went back to memorizing Hugo.

The result was that it took him on average 64 seconds to memorize a line. The 38 days of "practice" did not improve his ability to memorize lines of poetry.

Memory is not a muscle, practice does not make perfect when it comes to memory. Something else is needed and that something else is mnemonics, the subject of this book.

Another common misconception that deserves mention relates to the view that a trained memory remembers all.

At my public workshops, I am sometimes asked by a wide-eyed participant if after the seminar they will be able to remember everything they learned from that day forward. In this same vein, I have been asked to repeat verbatim a conversation I just had, or repeat, without variation something I had written.

When I answer "no" or fail to repeat the requested material, there is a look of disappointment and sometimes the suggestion that the systems then are somehow impractical.

The truth is that a trained memory will help you immeasurably in your personal and professional life, but it is not magic. Effort must always be expended. Your mind will not miraculously become an audio/video recording device with the mastery of the techniques presented here.

I cannot remember a conversation verbatim because I do not enter into that conversation for the purposes of remembering everything said exactly as I said it. I cannot remember precisely the words I chose in something that I've written because I did not apply my systems to that material.

This is not to say that I could not do so by applying the systems we will discuss and if there were a purpose in doing so.

The point is that when you are faced with a situation where the application of the techniques you will learn justify the time and effort you will expend, the results will be remarkable.

It should also be noted that there is no *one* best system for all applications of memory. I will introduce you to a number of systems and approaches that are very effective in dealing with various applications in your personal and professional life.

You will be taught a different technique for memorizing sequential data such as lists, than the system for remembering numbers, dates and appointments. The system for memorizing speeches and presentations that you will learn is different than the technique for remembering names and faces.

Indeed, your success in greatly improving your memory will depend to some extent on your ability to discern which system is appropriate to the material or task at hand.

One final myth I would like to discuss relates to the concept of the photographic memory.

Again, I seldom conduct a workshop where the question of "photographic memory" is not raised.

The classical photographic memory is something described as the innate ability to form "snapshot" like mental pictures of what the eye sees with great detail and with a minimum of conscious effort.

This "snapshot" may then later be examined mentally and recalled with great detail and accuracy.

I must tell you that it is my view that this type of mental behavior does not exist, or if it does exist, is far less common than is generally thought. It is so rare, in fact, each individual case is a significant scientific oddity.

In more than forty years of teaching memory to tens of thousands of people, I have never witnessed it.

I've met many people who have an exceptional ability to quickly assimilate information, as well as some who, with or without training, have learned to form quick and workable associations.

Kaavya Viswanathan the author of *How Opal Mehta Got Kissed, Got Wild, and Got a Life*, got herself in trouble when it was shown that she plagiarized 29 passages from the books of another novelist, Megan Viswanathan said she must have done so "unintentionally and unconsciously" as she has a photographic memory and never take notes.

Viswanathan is not the only plagiarist to claim unconscious influence from the depths of memory. Helen Keller lifted material verbatim from Margaret Canby's "The Frost Fairies" when writing her story "The Frost King" and more recently George Harrison claimed he did not intentionally rip of the Chiffons' "He's So Fine" when he wrote "My Sweet Lord." He said he had simply forgotten he had ever heard it.

In 1970, a Harvard scientist named Charles Stromeyer published a stunning paper in *Nature* about a Harvard student named Elizabeth, who could apparently perform astonishing feats of memory. Stromeyer designed a test where he covered Elizabeth's left eye and then showed her a pattern of 10,000 random dots.   The next day, he covered her right eye and then showed her another different 10,000 random dot pattern. Elizabeth was then able to mentally combine the two images to create *a random-dot stereogram* representing a three-dimensional image that appeared to float above the page.

Elizabeth seemed to provide conclusive proof that photographic memory is real and possible. Strangely however, Stromeyer married Elizabeth and she avoided any further testing.

A researcher named John Merritt tried to find someone like Elizabeth by publishing a photographic memory test in a number of magazines and newspapers. He hoped that someone would come forward with an ability similar to Elizabeth's. Roughly one million people took the test, and out of that number only 30 responded with the right answer. Merritt visited 15 of them in their homes but not one of them could pull off the trick with Merritt looking over their shoulder.

Does this mean that these people were dishonest or intentionally tried to mislead? Not at all. Does photographic memory exist? Again, I would say not at all.

There is a phenomenon often mistaken for a photographic memory called eidetic imagery.

Eidetic imagery is a strong after image that allows an individual an opportunity to replicate a scene in the conscious mind. The research indicates that eidetic imagery is found in approximately 5% of all children.

The research also shows, however, that the image can only be held for a short period of time, the accuracy is affected by the child's subjective state and this eidetic ability is almost always lost by puberty.

I view the idea of a photographic memory as somewhat disparaging, because it provides just another excuse for non-action. It implies that someone with a good memory possesses some natural ability we do not.

This is simply not true!

Chapter One

The Before Test

Before we begin your memory training, it is important for you to understand what your current abilities are, that is, how good or how bad you are at remembering different types of data.

Very few people understand these relative strengths and weaknesses because they have never given themselves a memory test, and for that reason they do not recognize the false limits they have learned to live with.

Some parts of this test may seem very difficult, even impossible. Yet these tasks are well within the capabilities of the human mind properly trained in a number of techniques.

Try your best in each section and adhere to the time limits given. Don't be concerned with poor performance; remember it is the purpose of this book to make memorization, such as demanded by the following tests both easy and enjoyable.

You will need a watch with a second hand to take this test.

You will be asked to memorize a number of different types of information and data before you will be asked to recall it. This is an important feature of the before test and this makes the test more analogous to real life applications.

When you are ready please turn the page and we will begin.

The Before Test
Part I – Sequential Information

Please take two minutes to memorize the following list in its precise order. When exactly **two minutes** are up – turn the page.

1. Rabbit	11. Dishwater
2. Book	12. Thursday
3. Boston	13. Coffee
4. Trudeau	14. Money
5. Satisfaction	15. Ice Cream
6. Suitcase	16. Elephant
7. Stethoscope	17. Olympics
8. Backpack	18. Railroad
9. Sunshine	19. Bandwidth
10. Memory	20. Toothpaste

The Before Test
Part II – Numerical Data

Please take two minutes to memorize all of the following dates in history and telephone numbers. When exactly **two minutes** are up – turn the page

First British Parliament	1295
Death Of Napoleon	1821
Pompeii Destroyed	79
Pilgrim's Landing	1620
Lindbergh's Flight	1927
Hundred Year War	1343 - 1453
Hitler Becomes Chancellor	1933
Harvard University Est.	1636
Battle Of Waterloo	1815
French Revolution	1789

Disneyland	662-7211
White House	456-1414
Oprah	876-2422
NBC New York	664-4444
House of Commons	486-0030
Library of Congress	996-1475
Sarah Palin	747-1812
Bellevue Hospital	562-1000
P.A. Douglas & Associates	444-8000
Irish Embassy	223-6281
David Letterman	232-9999

The Before Test
Part III – Complex Numbers

Please take three minutes to memorize the following set of numbers in such a way that if you were give the two-digit number to the left of the hyphen you could recount the six-digit number to the right of it.

30 - 420121

69 - 314781

25 - 968010

16 - 419217

47 - 850947

91 - 850151

13 - 224606

64 - 370774

89 - 897639

11 - 022460

12 - 123583

90 – 998752

19 – 285765

33 – 199908

29 – 232345

The Before Test
Part IV – Names & Faces

On the pages that follow you will be introduced to twenty people you have never seen before. Without writing anything down please try to memorize their names – first and last. You will have three minutes in total so you should not spend more than about 10 seconds per individual.

When you come to the last person, please stop before turning the page.

When you are ready to proceed, please turn the page.

Mr. Spade

Ms. Wydner

Ms. Washington

Dr. Toupin

Lighting Your Way To Excellence

Mrs. Pearson

Mr. Stone

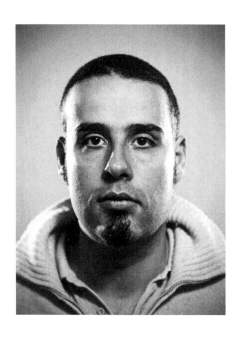

Mr. Mancuso

Mr. Masami

Mr. Stanley

Mr. Archer

The Answer Sheet
Part I – Sequential Information

Please take one minute <u>only</u> to enter in the spaces below the random list of twenty items you memorized in Part I of this before test. When exactly **one minute** is up – turn the page

1. _____   2. _____

3. _____   4. _____

5. _____   6. _____

7. _____   8. _____

9. _____   10. _____

11. _____   12. _____

13. _____   14. _____

15. _____   16. _____

17. _____   18. _____

19. _____   20. _____

The Answer Sheet
Part II – Numerical Data

Please take one minute <u>only</u> to enter in the spaces below the dates in history and telephone numbers you memorized in Part II of this before test. When exactly **one minute** is up – turn the page.

1. The Whitehouse Telephone? _____

2. Death of Napoleon? _____

3. Oprah's Telephone? _____

4. Battle of Waterloo? _____

5. Telephone at Disneyland? _____

6. Harvard University Established? _____

7. David Letterman's Telephone? _____

8. The Hundred Years' War? _____ to _____

9. Pilgrim's Landing? _____

10. P.A. Douglas & Associates Telephone? _____

The Answer Sheet
Part III – Complex Numbers

Please take one minute <u>only</u> to enter the six-digit number associated with the first ten complex number sets you were given in Part III.

1. **77** _____

2. **5** _____

3. **70** _____

4. **24** _____

5. **97** _____

6. **91** _____

7. **13** _____

8. **64** _____

9. **89** _____

10. **11** _____

The Answer Sheet
Part III – Names & Faces

In the spaces provided below and on the six pages that follow, please enter the first and last names of the people you met in Part III of this before test. When no more than **three minutes** are up – turn the page and score yourself on each section.

1. Name _____

2. Name   _____

3. Name   _____

4. Name _____

5. Name _____

6. Name   _____

7. Name   _____

8. Name _____

9. Name _____

10. Name _____

When you are finished, turn the page and score yourself

Score Sheet
Part I – Sequential Information

Please compare the following list to your answers on page 34. Give yourself two points for each correct response.

1. Rabbit	**2. Book**
3. Boston	**4. Trudeau**
5. Satisfaction	**6. Suitcase**
7. Stethoscope	**8. Backpack**
9. Sunshine	**10. Memory**
11. Dishwasher	**12. Thursday**
13. Coffee	**14. Money**
15. Ice Cream	**16. Elephant**
17. Olympics	**18. Railroad**
19. Bandwidth	**20. Toothpaste**

Score Sheet
Part II – Numerical Data

Please compare the following list to your answers on page 35. Give yourself two points for each correct date or telephone number.

1. The Whitehouse Telephone?	**456-1414**
2. Death of Napoleon?	**1821**
3. Oprah's Telephone?	**876-2422**
4. Battle of Waterloo?	**1815**
5. Telephone at Disneyland?	**662-7211**
6. Harvard University Established?	**1636**
7. David Letterman's Telephone?	**232-9999**
8. The Hundred Years' War?	**1343 - 1453**
9. Pilgrim's Landing?	**1620**
10. P.A. Douglas & Associates Telephone?	**444-8000**

Score Sheet
Part III – Complex Numbers

Please compare the following list to your answers on page 36. Give yourself two points for each correct six-digit response.

1.	77	-	284268
2.	5	-	417617
3.	70	-	916392
4.	24	-	226954
5.	97	-	604123
6.	91	-	001123
7.	13	-	224606
8.	64	-	370774
9.	89	-	897639
10.	11	-	022460

Score Sheet
Part IV – Names & Faces

Please compare the following list of first and last names to those you entered on pages 37 through 42. Give yourself one point for each correct first name and one point for each correct last name.

1. Mr. Stone

2. Mr. Stanley

3. Mr. Archer

4. Mr. Mancuso

5. Mr. Massami

6. Ms. Pearson

7. Mr. Toupin

8. Mr. Spade

9. Ms. Wydner

10. Ms. Washington

Score Sheet

Part I – Sequential Information   A) _____

Part II – Numerical Information   B) _____

Part III – Complex Numbers   C) _____

Part IV – Names & Faces   D) _____

Total (Percentage)   E) _____ %

The Before Test is out of 100 points so the score you have in (E) is also your percentage.

What Does Your Score Mean?

Well that was probably depressing. If you feel you did poorly, you are properly correct. There is some good news however and that is that you are not alone. The average score on this before test is less than 30%.

You received some bad news, that you are not perfect, at least not with regard to your current memory skills.

Now the good news, in the chapters that follow I will show you how to score 100% in each of these areas we have just tested and several

Chapter Two

Association

All memory is based on association. Everything that you now know, you know because at some point in your life, consciously, but more likely, subconsciously, you have formed an association between something new and something that you knew before. That's the way the human mind works. In literature the analogy is often drawn between a digital computer and the human mind. It's not a very good analogy. Human beings don't store information in bytes and locations, but rather, thoughts are interwoven and tied together.

Have you ever had the experience of hearing a song on the radio, a song that was maybe popular years ago when you were a high school student? When you hear that melody and you think to yourself, Oh, what was the title of that? What was the name of the group that sang that? Usually that information comes to you, but it doesn't come in isolation.

Rather, once you hear that song, the one that you haven't heard in so long, it brings back a lot of other memories as well, such as what your life was all about when that song was first popular; your boyfriend; your girlfriend; that summer. I think this underscores that the way our minds work, is through association.

I learned early in my life the importance of association because spelling was a real problem for me. Simple words that were never a problem for you, were a problem for me, words like believe; b-e-l-e-a-v-e. Or was it b-e-l-e-i-v-e? Or was it b-e-l-i-e-v-e?

Well, they all looked fine to me, and I kind of integrated these variations in my writing, but my teachers weren't impressed, they always wanted the same one, and the one in particular they liked was the one that had the i before e. They would say, Remember, Paul, it's i before e except after c, except in "neighbor" and "weigh" and "weird" . . . and eight million other exceptions. I felt like saying, if I could remember that, I could spell it.

It wasn't until a teacher said, "Listen, kid, if you want to remember how to spell that word, just remember you should never *believe a lie.*" Something clicked for me when the teacher said that. What the teacher was really saying was to associate the thing you're having difficulty with something that you do know.

Now, I wasn't that bad, I knew how to spell the word lie, and of course, in the correct spelling of the word believe, we have that little word lie, l-i-e. Piece of pie, is the same kind of thing.

Now, typically you've never had to do that, but I suggest to you that you've done the same thing in a myriad of ways to remember all nature of things.

If, for example, you have ever studied music, how did you first commit to your memory the notes of the treble clef: e, g, b, d, f Yes, every good boy deserves fudge or does fine. The notes that fell in between were easy as well because they formed a simple word: face, f-a-c-e.

If I asked you to pick up your pen and draw roughly the outline of the country Spain, could you do it? What about Germany; could you do it? What about Italy? Here you probably can come up with something reasonably close, because what does it look like? A boot.

How many years ago did you learn that? It was probably back in about Grade Three that a teacher said to you, "Students, what does this look like, what does this country look like?" And you all repeated, "It looks like a boot!"

Why have you remembered this all these years, because it's important? No, it's not important, how does that affect your life?

You have forgotten all kinds of important things throughout your life, but you have never forgotten the shape of the country Italy. Why, because it was a meaningful association, you and I tend to remember those things that we associate with other things. Association is the key because it is the way our minds normally function.

Acronyms allow us to associate information with the letters in common words. They act as cues.

HOMES reminds us of the five great lakes (Huron, Ontario, Michigan, Erie and Superior).

PATINA reminds us of the four major bodies of water (Pacific, Atlantic, Indian and arctic).

ACTS does the same for the four types of prayer in the Catholic Church (Adoration, Contrition, Thanksgiving and Supplication).

PAW helps us avoid explosions in the lab (Pour acid into water). Not the other way around.

SKILL cues us to the excretory organs of the body (Skin, Kidneys, Intestines, Liver and Lungs).

A PAIL holds the five types of wounds (Abrasion, Puncture, Avulsion, Incision and Laceration).

GUMP reminds us of the checklist before landing a propeller-drive airplane (Gas pumps on, Undercarriage down, Mixture rich and Prop full increase).

Acronyms are *more* than abbreviations. They are memory aids.

The advent of tweeting and text messaging has supplied a new lexicon unknown to most people out of their teens. These abbreviations simply make life easier in the 140-character universe:

BFF – Best Friends Forever

LOL – Laughing Out Loud

LTD – Living The Dream

ADBB – All Done Bye Bye

EWI – Emailing While Intoxicated

BIB – Boss is back

And my favorite:

POS – Parent Over Shoulder

When there is no single word available to remind us of that which we must recall, the acrostic was created. In an acrostic it is just the first letter in a phrase, sentence or rhyme that counts.

The acrostic has been used for centuries to help us recall fairly complex data. A few examples are:

George's Evening Lessons Never Dull

The Pentateuch

(Genesis, Exodus, Leviticus, Numbers, Deuteronomy)

Queen Victoria Can Eat Pie and Coffee

The Seven Hills of Rome

(Quirinal, Viminalm Capitoline, Esquiline, Palatine, Aretine, Coelian)

On Old Olympus Towering Top a Finn and German View some Hops

The Twelve Cranial Nerves

(Olfactory, Optic, Oculomotor, Trochlear, Trigeminal, Abducens, Facial, Acoustic, Glossopharyngeal, Vagus, Spinal Accessory, Hypoglossal)

Every Good Boy Deserves Fudge

The Notes of the Treble Clef

E, G, B, D, F

Practically Every Old Man Plays Poker Regularly

The Geological Ages

(Paleocene, Eocene, Oligocene, Miocene, Pliocene, Pleistocene, Recent)

Kangaroos Hop, Dancing Despite Coming Motherhood

The Metric Prefixes in Descending Order

(Kilo, Hecto, Deka, Deci, Centi, Milli)

King Phil Came Over for the Genes Special

Taxonomy Order

 (Kingdom, Phylum, Class, Order, Genus, Species)

Please Excuse My Dear Aunt Sally

The Order of Operations in Algebra

(Parenthesis, Exponents, Multiplication, Division, Addition, Subtraction)

Rhyming acrostics are even more effective:

Columbus Discovering America

> *In fourteen hundred and ninety-two,*
> *Columbus sailed the ocean blue.*

Day in the Month

> *Thirty days has September,*
> *April, June and November,*
> *All the rest have thirty-one,*
> *Except the second month we find,*
> *Has twenty-eight, 'til Leap Year gives it twenty-nine.*

Fair or Foul Weather

> *Red Sky in the morning,*
> *Sailors' warning,*
> *Red Sky at night,*
> *Sailors' delight*

The Phases of the Moon

>*When the moon doth form a C,*
>
>*It is decreasing hastily,*
>
>*But when the C's reversed, please note;*
>
>*It's getting full and soon will bloat.*

The Ten Commandments

>*Thou no God shall have but me;*
>
>*Before no idol bow thy knee;*
>
>*Take now the name of God in vain*
>
>*Nor dare the Sabbath day profane;*
>
>*Give both thy parents honor due;*
>
>*Take heed that thou no murder do;*
>
>*Abstain from words and deeds unclean*
>
>*Nor steal, though thou art poor and mean;*
>
>*Nor make a willful lie, nor love it.*
>
>*What is thy neighbor's do not covet.*

These devices, that is, the acronym and acrostic, are useful but require considerable time and thought to create, we need systems and techniques that we can apply quickly and on an ad hoc basis.

As the acronym and acrostic demonstrate the principle of association is highly useful and effective in providing the cues needed. But association in and of itself is really not enough.

You may have discovered that fact when you took the before test. You were asked to memorize twenty random items, perhaps you tried to make a story out of the list, but you found it wasn't enough. That is because association by itself is simply not enough.

The Mental Slap

In any mnemonic system or memory system, for it to help us at all, we have to couple this principle of association with another technique that I've called the mental slap.

In 1979 when I was writing the first edition of this book, I read everything I could get my hands on the subject of memory and concentration, I found that the very best things written were not written by our contemporaries, psychologists, writers, or thinkers of today, rather, the very best things written on the topic of memory were written by the ancients, people like Hypocrites and Socrates and Aristotle. Those people had to have good memories; they had to know how the human mind works with regard to memory. They didn't have all the devices in hand that you and I have: pens, and papers, and Dictaphones and computers.

I think it was from the translation of a writing by Aristotle, this great teacher, where I got this principle that I've referred to as the mental slap. Aristotle was talking about an experience he had in class one day and how he found that as he was presenting the crux of his argument, the thing that he wanted that student to remember always, he thought if he, just kind of reached across the desk and slapped that student as hard as he could, he thought, that student will never forgot that experience. They remembered for the rest of their lives that day in class when, for no apparent reason, the teacher knocked them off their chair.

Now, I'm not suggesting this as a system for remembering names, but mentally we can do the same thing through the creation of pictures in our mind that stand out, that are indelible, that can't be forgotten. What I'm really asking you to do is to draw more on the right side of your brain and less on the left.

We have known for hundreds of years that we really have two brains, at least we have two hemispheres within our brain, and they're really quite separate and distinct, they're really only joined at one place, and that's the corpus callosum. It's through the corpus callosum that all signals and transmissions travel from one hemisphere of the brain to the other.

We've known as well for some time that the left side of the brain controls the right side of the body and, conversely, that the right controls the left. We've mainly discovered that through the study of stroke patients. If someone suffers a massive stroke and they've survived that stroke and if the stroke comes in the right hemisphere of their brain, we've noted that the impairment will always be to the left side of their body, if the stroke is to the left side of their brain, the impairment will be to the right. Nothing new there, but what *is* new and why Roger Sperry at Harvard University, won the Nobel Prize in Medicine in 1981 was that he was able to show us categorically that the left side of the brain controls different types of cognitive functioning than the right.

When you're being logical, when you're being reasonable, when you're being rational, when you're adding up your checkbook, when you're verbalizing as I now am, then you're drawing very much on the left side of your brain, because that's the side that controls reason and rationality, but when you're being imaginative or creative, when you're seeing pictures laid out spatially in your mind, then you're drawing very much on the right hemisphere within your brain.

Now, you and I have been brought up and educated and socialized pretty much in a left-biased society, from the time you were a fairly young child, your parents, your teachers, and society have said what to you, don't be silly, think along these parameters, and that's good, it's got our society where it is today. We are a very rational people, but there is a cost, and the cost is in terms of the further development of your right brain.

Like many people reading this book, you probably haven't used your imagination from the time you were a fairly young child, I'm going to ask you to draw back on that skill and ability that you do have. It's in the background.

If you have a young child or know a boy or girl under age nine or ten, do they have a good imagination? They have a great imagination. When you read or tell them a story, they are in the place in the moment.

But as adults we feel it is foolish to live in the fanciful world of imagination. We take too literally the admonition found in Corinthians *"When I was a child, I spake as a child, I understood as a child, I thought as a child: but when I became a man, I put away childish thing."*

What a shame. If we didn't have men and women with imagination we wouldn't have the airplane, or television or the Internet or the polio vaccine or IPhones or Facebook.

You see it is through the use of your imagination that you make things stand out. You probably can't remember much from the time you were three or four or five, but I would bet you could remember some event or occurrence from those years.

Think about it for a moment what do you recall?

When I ask this question at my memory seminars I typically get answers like, "I remember breaking my arm" or "I remember my little brother coming home from the hospital" or "I remember when my dog bit me."

I was born in Ireland and emigrated from there when I was five, so this event must have occurred when I was four or five. I remember see a little friend of mine being struck and killed outside my front door. I can also remember the funeral. In those days in that place the corpse was laid out on a table in the parlor, surrounded by candles and flowers.

I can still see the little follow lying there and the women dressed in black, even the smell of what I thought was wilting flowers but was embalming fluid. I have had occasion to smell it since and it still evokes these strong images.

What do these memories have in common? They represent events that were dramatic or traumatic in some way. An injury, the appearance of a new family member and the disruption that causes in a child's life, the whole ritual of death.

You probably drive a car every day but you can't recall each day you drove your car. But you remember the day you had a car accident.

You don't remember every time you have sex, but you remember the first time.

It's waiting in abeyance, if, at the same time, you can formulate associations using the techniques I'll share with you, you're going to find as I now have that not only is it easy to remember, it's impossible to forget. My problem now literally is not forgetting things; it's trying to forget certain things and not being able to.

Let me show you now by taking this principle of association and this other concept that we've referred to so far as the mental slap, which is really nothing more than imagination, and put them together in such a way that it can help us to recall information that perhaps otherwise we might have some difficulty recalling.

Nuns and Airplanes

The following is a list of ten random and unrelated items.

Tree

Airplane

Envelope

Nuns

Motorcycle

Supermarket

Fire

Teapot

Mouse

Book

As we go through this list, I want you to make some mental pictures. I want you to see, first of all, a tree and an airplane in your mind's eye, I want you to see it, not think about it, I want you to actually see the image of the tree and the airplane.

But you know, if you were to park an airplane, an aircraft, at your local airport sitting beside a tree, if that were the image you were to create, you would probably forget it, that's too ordinary, that's too everyday, that's too banal and our mind tends to sweep that kind of nonsense away.

I want you to reverse the roles of the tree and the airplane, I don't want you to see an airplane flying through the sky, I want you to see a tree flying through the sky.

Now, I know that's crazy; that's goofy; that's impossible. It may be impossible, but it's not impossible for you to see it, you can see anything in your mind's eye. I want you to see the image of the tree flying through the sky. Make it more absurd, put wings on the tree, carve windows out of the trunk, put a Southwestern Airlines symbol on the roots, but see it, picture it. It's not how long you see it; it's the clarity of the image, if you can see it clearly in your mind's eye for a split second, you've got it.

Let's go on, the next association I want you to make is between an airplane and an envelope, but, again, if you were to picture the envelope lying on the seat of the aircraft, you would forget that, that's too ordinary, that's too every day, that's too banal. Start with an airplane sitting on the apron of the tarmac but not covered by a hangar or a building of that sort, rather, it's covered by a gigantic envelope. Envelopes are sized by number - #9, #10, number, well this is a number 10 million envelope covering this jumbo jet, see it.

Let's go on, envelope and nuns, see yourself holding open a large manila envelope, and millions of little nuns are being poured into it, little baby nuns all wearing little black-and-white habits. Can you see that, maybe it's a window envelope, and the nuns are all pushed up against the plastic; trying to get out, see that in your mind's eye.

Let's go on, nuns and motorcycle, just bringing those two together conjures up all kinds of absurd images. We're not going to picture a young nun dressed in civvies riding a Honda in Paraguay, rather, what we're going to see is an older nun wearing the most traditional black-and-white habit nuns have ever worn, riding a Harley, see that in your mind's eye, she's doing wheelies up and down in front of your house, picture that, see it.

Let's go on, motorcycle and supermarket, you're in the supermarket - Safeway, or Alpha Beta, or A&P, shopping for your groceries, but people aren't pushing these little tin carts around like they normally do, rather, they're all riding motorcycles.

As you come into the store, you're given one of these large, heavy bikes, and you're expected to drive down the aisle with one hand and pluck off your groceries with the other, and you're not doing a very effective job. You're bumping into things, you're falling off, the fumes are rising. Can you see the bedlam of that scene? See yourself involved in that situation in the supermarket, on your motorcycle, but make sure that you see you in the picture.

Supermarket and fire, you're at the checkout counter ready to pay for your groceries, but all of the sudden the clerk gets a strange look in her eyes, and she turns on her heels and she's gone. You think, "Well, that was kind of rude, I wonder why she did that."

And then as you turn, you see the reason why: The store is on fire! It's like the burning of Atlanta, there are explosions, the roof is caving in, Mr. Redenbacher's popcorn is going off. You have to dive through the window to save yourself. Picture that in your mind's eye: trapped in the fire at the supermarket.

See it. the firemen run in, but they're not carrying these great hoses they normally carry. Rather, they're carrying little porcelain teapots, they're trying to douse the flames with these little teapots full of water, and they're not doing a very effective job, they're like the Keystone Cops running back and forth, tripping over one another. See that in your mind's eye, picture that: the firemen trying to douse the flames with these teapots full of water.

Teapot and mouse, your company, your department is hosting a very important function, there's going to be a number of dignitaries from the community there, your boss is going to be in attendance, there's going to be other senior officials from your organization, local, state, provincial politicians, federal politicians will be there. The Queen of England will be in attendance.

Your boss has asked you if you wouldn't mind consenting to pour tea for the group this evening and you agree to do this.

The queen walks up to you and says, "Can I have a cup of tea?" You say, "Of course." But as you pick up this teapot and try to pour her a cup of tea, nothing comes out, she looks rather puzzled, as are you. As you set the teapot down and lift the lid together at the same time, you see why nothing came out: There's a dead mouse inside clogging the drain! Well, of course you pull it up by the tail, hurl it against the wall, and ask Her Majesty, "Now, is this one lump or two?" Can you see the embarrassment of finding this dead mouse in the teapot at this particularly important function, see that in your mind's eye.

Finally, mouse and book, you're in a church, you're in a library, you're being very, very still and quiet, reverent, so still, in fact, that a little mouse starts to creep up the book. You give it a chance, of course, to get about halfway up, and then you silently slip your hands behind both covers, and you slam it shut, and as you do so, you can hear its little bones cracking as you turn that mouse into your bookmark, again see it in your mind's eye.

Let me give you a moment to go back and see if you can't recall, I'll give you the first one to get you going, and there's a reason why I have to do that. The first word is the word tree, think about what you associated in your mind with tree. What was the other side of the picture, when you think of the first word in our random list write it down.

Then having written down the second word on the list, think of your next association, write down the third item and so on and so on until you have got all ten. Turn the page now and replicate the list.

List No. 1

1. _____ **TREE** _____

2. _____

3. _____

4. _____

5. _____

6. _____

7. _____

8. _____

9. _____

10. _____

How did you do, were you able to get them all? Was it difficult?

Is this a system, no, it's not; it's not a system because for one thing it simply takes too long. Also, you could not jump around in the list. If I were to ask you what number seven was, could you could not instantly provide the answer, rather you would have to work your way through the list, tree, airplane, nuns, motorcycle and so on until you got to the number seven.

I gave you this little exercise to demonstrate the importance of the two key components that we'll find in all mnemonic or memory systems, these are the two essential building blocks:

ASSOCIATION
IMAGINATION

It is imagination that really forms the basis of the mental slap, shortly I will show you a number of actual systems that will assist you in remembering lists, numbers, speeches as well as names and faces. You will learn to recall any type of information, abstract and concrete. But this in itself was not a system; I gave you this exercise simply to demonstrate the importance of the two key components that we'll find in all mnemonic or memory system - association and imagination.

We will learn to put those blocks together in various and different ways to help us to remember the information and data every manager and executive must recall: sequential and financial data, the names of client, customers, staff and colleagues. There will be systems that will assist you in preparing and delivering speeches and giving presentations. But before I show you the first real and practical mnemonic system, the Peg System, I would like to introduce the concept of learning styles, as it impacts greatly on the success you will have with this system as well as other systems we will discuss in this book.

Learning Styles

Some people have no trouble with exercises like the one we just completed. Others have some difficulty. I believe these differences stems from the fact that we do not all have the same learning style.

There are three learning styles and while it is true that most people engage all three, it is also true that each of us has a favored style. Understanding your learning style can have profound influence on your ability to learn, remember and recall. The three learning styles are:

Auditory Learners

Auditory learners learn best by listening and engaging in conversation. They are keenly aware of, and tend to remember, things that they hear. They are good storytellers and they enjoy talking rather than writing. They enjoy music and recognize subtle nuances others miss. They are also good with words and language. Auditory learners learn best when they can hear the information. Since they acquire knowledge by reading aloud, verbal repetition is an effective means of study for the auditory learner. Audio Learners make up 35% of the population.

Visual Learners

Visual learners learn best by seeing what they are being taught. Visualization is natural to them. They have a good sense of direction almost a built in GPS and prefer maps to verbal or written directions. They may have trouble remembering verbal instructions unless they are also written down. They prefer to read information from a textbook or blackboard rather than listen to a lecture. They may be visually artistic and may tend to draw and doodle. You may catch them closing their eyes when trying to remember something. Visual Learners make up 65% of the population.

Kinesthetic Learners

Kinesthetic learners learn best by doing particularly through movement, they are drawn to and are typically good at sports, dance and other physical activities. Their hands-on approach attracts them to experiential learning situations such as role-plays and other simulations. They are uncomfortable in classrooms settings that lack opportunities for hands-on experience. They tend to get a little "antsy" during long lectures. They remember what was done more than what was said. Kinesthetic Learners make up just 5% of the population.

According to researchers at the National Institute for Development and Administration at the University of Texas, we tend to remember:

> 10% of what we read
> 20% of what we hear
> 30% of what we see

This research is not surprising considering the proportion of the population that is visual minded. An interesting statistic is that they found that people also tend to remember 50% of what they hear and see and 90% of what they do and say, the implication then is that the more senses you can involve in the learning experience, the better.

Please take a moment to determine your individual learning style by completing the following quiz:

Learning Style Quiz

Instructions: For each of the following twenty questions, please circle the response that you feel BEST describes your preference or behavior MOST often:

1. In terms of leisure activities, I prefer to:

    a) Listen to music, talk on the telephone or attend a musical
    b) Read or go to the movies
    c) Go for a walk, exercise, garden, cook or build something

2. When attempting to learn something new, I prefer to:

    a) Have someone show me or teach me
    b) Read how to do it myself
    c) Try to figure it out by doing myself

3. I tend to be most distracted by:

    a) Sounds and noises
    b) Movement and untidiness
    c) Activities taking place around me

4. When meeting someone for the second time, I am more likely to:

    a) Remember their name and what we talked about previously
    b) Likely forget their name but recognize their face
    c) Remember what we did together

5. At a social function or party, I like to:

   a) Listen mostly or maybe talk with one or two people at a time
   b) Observe how everyone looks and "people watch"
   c) Dance or take part in some activity

6. When I cook a new dish, I usually:

   a) Follow the recipe
   b) Call my mother (or another) for help
   c) Follow my instincts or experiment

7. I like a teacher who:

   a) Uses the lecture method and is a good speaker
   b) Writes on the chalkboard or who uses a PowerPoint
      presentation effectively
   c) Designs experiential activities that get the class involved

8. My emotions are shown mainly through:

   a) Voice
   b) Facial expression
   c) Body language

9. When driving, I:

    a) Turn on the radio as soon as I get in the car

    b) Like to enjoy the peace and quiet

    c) Move around and stop often so as not to get tired

10. When shopping for a new outfit, I tend to:

    a) Imagine how I would look in it

    b) Ask the sales clerk how I look in it

    c) Try it on and see how it looks on me

11. When buying a new car, I would likely:

    a) Read what Consumer Reports has to say about it

    b) Discuss my needs with my friends

    c) Test drive a number of different models

12. I know when communicating with others, I tend to:

    a) Vary my tone and pitch

    b) Have animated facial expression and speak with my eyes

    c) Gesture and use may hands

13. Which of these three best describes you?

    a) I like to talk with people
    b) I like solitude
    c) I like to move, dance or exercise

14. My first memory as a child, is of me:

    a) Seeing or witnessing something
    b) Someone saying something to me
    c) Doing something

15. I remember things best by:

    a) Recording careful notes and instructions
    b) Saying things out loud and repeating things
    c) Doing things, practicing the activity

16. Which of the following do you say most often?

    a) "I see what you are saying"
    b) "I hear what you are saying"
    c) "I know how you feel"

17. When ordering from menu in a restaurant, I usually:

   a) Picture what the food would look like
   b) Talk about the choices with my dining companion
   c) Image how the food will taste like

18. I form my opinion of other people more from:

   a) What they look like
   b) What they say
   c) How they make me feel

19. When I am in troubled or worried, I usually:

   a) Focus of the of worst-case scenario
   b) Talk to someone about how I feel
   c) Do something to deal with the situation or do something to
      take my mind of it.

20. Which for the following statements is MOST true for you?

   a) I follow written directions better than oral directions
   b) I follow oral directions better than written directions
   c) I prefer to just figure things out myself by doing them

Scoring & Interpretation

Add up the number of times you circled the letter "A," the number of times you circled the letter "B" and the number of times you circled the letter "C." The letter that you circled most often indicates your learning style. If you circled the letter "A" most often, then your learning style is Auditory, if the letter "B" was circled most often your learning style is Visual and if the letter "C" was circled more often then your learning style is Kinesthetic.

Determining Your Style

	SCORE	LEARNING STYLE
A =		
B =		
C =		

Memory Implications
of Learning Style

Most mnemonics systems take a visual approach to learning. Visualization
is at the heart of most systems. In mnemonics we attempt to make visually
notable and memorable mental pictures. If you are an auditory or
kinesthetic learner you may find this emphasis on imagery unnatural.

Obviously Visual Learners can embrace the techniques more readily, but
this does not mean that mnemonic excellence is unavailable to Audio and
Kinesthetic Learners.

Audio and Kinesthetic Learners need to modify the mnemonic approach
to suit their learning styles. If you are an auditory learner, you will want to
use auditory cues to create your mnemonics. If you are a Kinesthetic
Learner, you will want to imagine performing actions or using tools as the
basis of your mnemonic techniques.

Short vs. Long-Term Memory

You are reading this book to hopefully improve your long-term memory.

You want to be able to read something and not just make it through that meeting that you're attending and then forget it all, you want to be able to apply that information in your organizational life. You want to be able to study for that examination not just to find that shortly after you passed the test, you forgot it all. You want to be able to meet someone, hear the name, lock it onto that face. And even if you don't see them for another six months, when you do, you want to be able to call that name back and be able to use it instantly.

All information coming into our conscious or our subconscious minds through any of our sense organs first of all goes through a perceptual screen that for lack of a better term, I've called short-term memory, or STM.

At that stage of the game, ninety-nine percent of everything you will ever know will be forever forgotten, now, that's not altogether dysfunctional, it certainly is a problem, but it's not totally dysfunctional. If you and I had the ability to remember everything always, we couldn't think, we couldn't survive. If you could remember for the rest of your life every trivial conversation you've ever had, every sitcom you watched on television, every street noise you heard as you drove to work in the morning, you wouldn't be able to see the forest from the trees.

The problem, however, is one of discernment, many important things that you would like to recall are also washed away at short term because you don't have systems in place that enable you to move them into long-term memory.

Consider this model:

Long vs. Short-Term Memory

You see, once information is in long-term memory, it is there to stay. The problem most of us have is getting information into long-term memory. Our short-term memories are also extremely limited, both in terms of the amount of information we can hold at one time and the length of time that we can hold it in short term.

Let me prove that to you, on the next page you will find four numbers labeled **A** through **D**. Read the six-digit number labeled **A** below as you normally would, then immediately turn the page and enter it into the corresponding space. You will not likely have any problem with this six-digit number. Next do the same thing with the seven-digit number, that is, read the number, turn the page and enter it. Then follow the same procedure for the eighth and ninth digit numbers.

Long vs. Short-Term Memory

A) 6 1 0 7 2 3

B) 2 1 7 4 3 8 6

C) 5 2 7 1 7 5 3 2

D) 7 6 9 1 0 1 3 4 7

Read each number, one at a time, then IMMEDIATELY turn the page and enter it in the corresponding place:

Long vs. Short-Term Memory

A) __ __ __ __ __ __

B) __ __ __ __ __ __ __

C) __ __ __ __ __ __ __ __

D) __ __ __ __ __ __ __ __ __

Have a look at the results. Did you find that the six and seven digit numbers were not a problem but the eight and nine digit numbers were a challenge?

That is your short-term memory. The average person can only recall seven bits of information at a time. It is for that reason that telephone numbers were initially set at seven digits.

Without looking back, enter the first six-digit number in the space below:

A) __ __ __ __ __ __

Were you able to do it, probably not?

This is your short-term memory. Not only can we only hold six or seven items in our short-term memory at a time, but we can only hold it for a matter of seconds. Your short-term memory is limited both in terms of the amount of information it can hold and the length of time it can hold it, it's like a slate, when you went from the first number to the second, you wiped the slate clean. When you went from the second to the third, you wiped the second number. That is your short-term memory, extremely limiting, we need to stop relying on our short-term memory, we need to develop systems to help us recall the myriad of information and data we experience every day.

When I meet you, I've got fifteen to twenty seconds to transfer your name into my long-term memory, if I can't do it in that time, I won't remember your name.

When you're reading and you come across an idea or concept that you want to recall, if you don't have a system in place that will allow you to almost instantly lock in on that information and transfer it from short to long-term memory, you're not going to recall it, you're not going to remember it, you're going to read on, and something else is going to capture your imagination. You've gone, in a sense, from the first number to the second. The first thought, like the first number, was wiped from the slate. Our short-term memories are not reliable.

I have people say to me that they could hold information in their short-term memory much longer than twenty seconds; no they can't, not at least without recitation. It is like they have the information in a holding pattern.

The example is where I look a number up in a telephone book, but the book is on a chain, so as I talk over to the telephone, I recite the number, 4-2-3-5-7-5-6, 4-1-3-5-7-5-6. As long as I keep reciting the number I am fine, I can even punch out the numbers on the phone, but if it rings busy – it's back to the book!

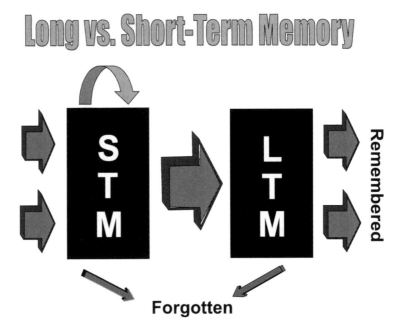

Now, I can't do anything directly to enhance your short or your long-term memory, your ability in both those areas is set by genetics and other factors and it's unchangeable. But in memory training, we don't focus on either improving our long or short-term memories. What we do is we focus our attention on providing skills and techniques, systems that will enable you, while information is in short term, to encode it and get it into your long-term memory, once it's in your long-term memory, it's there to stay. The difficulty that we're having, the problem that most people have, is how do you get it in.

Experience has shown that one way in which we might facilitate the transfer of information into our long-term memories is by the development of what we might think of as the mnemonic equivalent of a filing cabinet. Think of it, we can't hold in our minds, for example, all of the information associated with each of our clients or customers: their purchase history, contact information, credit standing, et cetera, but by filing the information on each of our clients alphabetically or in some other logical way in our filing cabinets, all we need to know is their name, and we can quickly retrieve all of this data, it really comes down to a series of cues.

There are, however several factors that influence our ability to recall encoded information, that is memory that has made it into long-term memory.

The Seven Deadly Sins of Memory

This seems like an appropriate time to discuss the seven features of human memory that, while functional, can interfere with our ability to recall accurately in a timely manner.

These "memory malfunctions" can be divided into seven categories or "sins." The first three are in a sense sins of omission insofar as they interfere with our recall of the information altogether whereas the last four might be views as sins of commission inasmuch as they result in inaccuracies, inconsistencies or a lack of fidelity in what is recalled.

Transience

Transience simply refers to the fact that memories tend to fade over time. We tend to remember recent events more vividly than events that occurred the distant past.

Blocking

Blocking refers to retrieval interference of encoded information resulting in temporary inaccessibility or what we often refer to as the "Tip of the Tongue" experience.

Absent-mindedness

This memory dysfunction refers to problems occurring at the interface or memory and attention. We have all experienced it, the misplacement of our car keys, eyeglasses, wallet etc. The cause is a lack of attention at the time the information is encoded.

Misattribution

Misattribution is the first of the "Seven Deadly Memory Sins" where we recall information or events accurately but where we inaccurately recall the source of the information. For example, a person who witnesses a robbery may blame the crime on something he saw on a television program.

Suggestibility

Suggestibility refers to the situation where memories are influenced or clouded by external factors. For example, a witness to a crime remembers the perpetrator as white but after watching television reports that the perpetrator was African American he then "remembers" he was black.

Bias

Bias is similar to the sin of suggestibility inasmuch as an individual's preconceptions, prejudices or worldview distort the memory. An example of Bias might be when at the death of a parent, a religiously pious son might remember with great fondness a deep religious childhood that did not exist at least at the level they recall.

Persistence

Persistence refers to the unwanted recall of information that is troubling or disturbing. Persistence is common when an individual has experienced a significant trauma, such as a rape or molestation or other violent crime.

Absent-mindedness

The third "deadly sin" warrants further comment. According to John Orberg author of the books, *When the Game is Over It All Goes Back in the Box* we spend (or more accurately waste) roughly sixteen minutes a day looking for our lost possessions. It's a sin we are all guilty of: forgetting where we left the TV remote, or our glasses or our car keys, even where we parked our car.

Sometimes it's something more important than the TV remote. Yo Yo Ma, the famed cellist, tells the story about getting into a cab in New York and putting his $2.5 million cello in the trunk. Arriving at his destination, he pays the cabbie, gets out of the cab, and walks off, leaving his cello in the trunk, not realizing until he gets into the hall what he had done.

Some people are plagued by misplaced treasures. My wife loves it when I tell the story of how she put a $20,000 ring in such a good hiding place that she never saw it again.

The term *absent-mindedness* is an altogether appropriate name for this phenomenon because our minds' concentration is focused elsewhere, and not at the task at hand. If we can understand the causes of absent-mindedness, then maybe we can eliminate it or at least greatly reduce its significance.

The first cause of absent-mindedness is how much attention we're paying at the crucial moment. And the other involves how deeply we encode information.

The is a famous film clip that often shows up in psychology 101 in which students are asked to watch a video of people passing a basketball between each other, and they are asked to count the number of passes. Then when it is finished the participants are asked if they noticed anything unusual in the clip. Most of the students are rather puzzled by the question and say no. Then the experimenter replays the video clip but this time without having to focus on counting the passes everyone see a person dressed like a gorilla walk right through the scene, it even smiles at the camera.

To a large extend absent-mindedness is a result of sensory overload. We live in a multitasking society where too many things are happening at the same time and not surprisingly some of these things fall between the cracks. And the older we become, and the busier we get with our careers and our families, the worse it becomes.

The second element cause of absent-minded relates to the depth at which we process information. If the encoding is too shallow it will not take. Many people simply do not know how to increase the depth of focus.

Many people confuse absent-mindedness with a poor memory but they are really two different things. Nonetheless memory training can help us deal with absent-mindedness caused by either the lack of original awareness or the depth of focus.

Obviously since the cause of much of our absent-mindedness is the lack of original awareness, the solution is to increase and focus that awareness. One way to do this is to tell yourself as you put the car keys on the coffee table, "I am putting my keys on the coffee table." Or, as you leave your car in the car park, "I am parked by the exit door on the fourth floor." Better yet is to actually visualize the car keys on the coffee table. When you place your glasses on the refrigerator, see a huge set of glasses on the refrigerator.

A physical reminder can also help. If you don't want to forget to drop a letter in the mail on the way to work, set it by the door. Hang your suit on the door so you can't go through it without remembering to take it to the dry cleaners. "Have a place for everything and put everything in its place" is still good advice. If you waste a lot of time looking for your keys, hang a hook by the front door and get in the habit of hanging them up as soon as you come in.

The problem of absent-mindedness is one of inattention; your mind is literally absent when you perform a particular action. Overcome this annoyance by increasing your original awareness.

Other Impediments to Memory

In addition to the seven deadly sins of memory shown above, there are a number of other environmental factors and behavioral choices that have been shown to negatively affect the proper functioning of your brain.

Stress

Stress is the spice of life. It energizes and can motivate us to do our best but too much stress or chronic, continuous stress can be highly destructive. A great deal of work has been done on the effects of stress on memory and it all indicates a negative inverse relationship. Simply stated, stress is also the enemy of memory. As stress increases, our ability to acquire, retain and recall information decreases. Long-term stress actually results in hippocampal atrophy or a shrinking hippocampus, the gland that determining what will be remembered and what will not.

Information Overload

Another impediment to memory, not unrelated to stress, is information overload. The term "Information overload" is a term popularized by Alvin Toffler the author of "Future Shock," and speaks to the effect of the bombardment overwhelming information on one's ability to absorb information. Emails, faxes, cell phones, the Internet, Facebook, Twitter, the 500 channel universe. All of these things act as distractions.

The average American was exposed to approximately 500 advertisements a day in 1970. Today, that number has increased to well over 3000. Technology is changing so rapidly that you must master new technologies every few months just to stay up to date and you probably meet more people in a month than your grandparents met in a year.

It's not hard to see why people today have trouble than ever remembering. We are constantly being bombarded with information and data, some of it useful and relevant, much of it not, and it is becoming progressively more difficult to separate the two.

Drugs and Alcohol

Because of the relative prevalence of impaired driving there has been considerable research done into the impact of alcohol on the brain's motor functions such as operating an automobile. These studies have shown that not only does alcohol have a negative effect on our driving but they also show that even as little as two or three drinks taken four times a week lowers our ability to perform many thinking tasks including remembering.

There was a popular television commercial a few years back that shows a shirtless young man awaking after a night of obvious partying and heavy drinking who, after checking everything out, is relieved to find that he is fine. As he gets out of bed however, the camera zooms in on the football-sized tattoo on his back. Humorous but actually true, people who alternate between sobriety and intoxication find that things learned in one state are difficult to remember in the other.

Smoking

Anything that impairs oxygen supply to the brain, as smoking does, negatively affects optimum functioning. In a recent study on smoking conducted by researchers at the University of Michigan it was found that smoking impairs our ability to think just like alcohol. It was shown that smoking of cigarettes has a negative impact on our memory and our problem-solving skills.

Lack of Sleep and Fatigue

If you have ever gone several nights with very little or no sleep, you know how it affects your overall performance. Numerous studies have shown that too little sleep can negatively impact our ability to form new memories, not only has lack of sleep been linked to short-term memory loss, but also the lack of quality sleep reduces our ability to focus our concentration. This is crucial because our inability to concentrate is fundamental to memory. Memory is the art of concentration.

That Reminds Me

In my house, every Christmas my family would watch Frank Capra's, "It's a Wonderful Life." If you are familiar with the classic, you will recall the scene when Uncle Billy has lost the Savings and Loan deposit. The camera pans down to his hand, which has two strings, tied around his fingers.

The strings were to remind him not to forget something. The string was to "keep" the thought there, to be remembered later.

All mnemonic systems are really variations on this theme.

One of the earliest recorded cueing methods was the loci method; a location system first developed by the Greeks and, like many things, was later adopted by the Romans. Loci, is the plural of locus and means place or location. The principle behind the Loci method is that we can best remember places we are familiar with. It developed from the correct assumption that if we associate something we wish to remember with a place we know well, the location will serve as a cue to our recall.

We know through his writings that Cicero used this system, this great orator was able to give a speech that may have lasted for several hours, covering precisely the points that he hoped to address in the exact order that they should be addressed by associating each of the thoughts in his speech with a part of his home. Cicero tells us that the poet Simonides developed this system. As the story goes Simonides was entertaining a large group of wealthy noblemen when two mysterious strangers called him outside. As he left the banquet hall, the roof suddenly collapsed crushing everyone inside beyond recognition. It was impossible to identify the dead until Simonides stepped up and identified everyone according to where they were sitting.

Simonides came to the realization that it would be possible to remember anything by associating it with an image of a loci or location. And so the Loci method was born. A system, incidentally, that was utilized by learned people into the 1600's when it was largely replaced by phonetic systems.

How did the Loci method work?

Let me give you an example. First, I have to establish a series of loci or locations to which I could associate my thoughts or perhaps the items on a list.

The most common loci or locations used were the rooms or other features in the Roman's own home. For example my first loci might be my front door, my second loci might be the foyer, the third a staircase, the forth my conservatory, the fifth the kitchen, then the bedroom and so on.

I might have twenty or thirty or more locations in my home, Cicero tells us he had several hundred. As I use these same locations time and again and can easily take a mental tour of these familiar places, it becomes very easy to recall.

If, as an ambitious young Roman, I wanted to recall all the items on my "to do" list I would simply visually associate each of these items with a place in my home.

Consider the following "to do" list:

Aurelius' List

1. Have my toga cleaned

2. Attend Christian/Lion match at the coliseum

3. Pickup barrel of vino

4. Buy a new slave

5. Meet Claudius at the baths

6. Check out the Chariot races at Circus Maximus

To remember the first item on my list, I might see my expensive new toga nailed to my front door. As I step through the doorway a lion pounces at me. As I look up the staircase a barrel of wine rolls down toward me and I have to jump out of the way. Having climbed the staircase to the conservatory I find a beautiful new slave standing on a box for my inspection. As I walk into the kitchen I find Claudius taking a bath in the sink. Opening the door to the bedroom, I find a chariot has replaced my bed.

Read the above paragraph one more time, seeing each image in your own mind, and then turn the page.

Fill in the blanks by taking a mental tour of "your" house:

1. **Front Door** _____

2. **Foyer** _____

3. **Staircase** _____

4. **Conservatory** _____

5. **Kitchen** _____

6. **Bedroom** _____

Cicero tells us that he used this system to deliver long speeches with great success. Not only did the Romans not have the devices we have today to help us - pens, paper, computers, index cards and Teleprompters, but it was also considered unacceptable for a learned man to refer to notes when speaking.

How could the Loci System be applied to speeches?

Let's use Mark Antony's famous speech to the senate after the death of Julius Caesar (Act 3, Scene 2) from Shakespeare's play:

Friends, Romans, countrymen, lend me your ears;
I come to bury Caesar, not to praise him;
The evil that men do lives after them,
The good is oft interred with their bones,

So let it be with Caesar ... The noble Brutus
Hath told you Caesar was ambitious:
If it were so, it was a grievous fault,
And grievously hath Caesar answered it ...
Here, under leave of Brutus and the rest,
(For Brutus is an honourable man;
So are they all; all honourable men)
Come I to speak in Caesar's funeral ...
He was my friend, faithful and just to me:
But Brutus says he was ambitious;
And Brutus is an honourable man....
He hath brought many captives home to Rome,
Whose ransoms did the general coffers fill:
Did this in Caesar seem ambitious?
When that the poor have cried, Caesar hath wept:
Ambition should be made of sterner stuff:
Yet Brutus says he was ambitious;
And Brutus is an honourable man.

To deliver this speech Mark Antony would choose a mental picture to represent his first thought.

Friends, Romans, countrymen, lend me your ears;

It might be ears. In which case I would see a huge ear nailed to his front door.

I come to bury Caesar, not to praise him;

Mark might use the image of a coffin to represent this thought. As he steps into the foyer of his home, he finds a coffin there.

The evil that men do lives after them,
The good is oft interred with their bones,

As he looks up his staircase he sees human bones scattered on the stairs.

Now when this Roman steps before the senate, he doesn't draw a blank. He simply takes a mental tour of his home. He sees his from door and finds an ear nailed to it, reminding him of:

Friends, Romans, countrymen, lend me your ears;

Stepping over the threshold into the foyer he finds a coffin there:

I come to bury Caesar, not to praise him;

Looking up his staircase he sees bone scattered thereon:

The evil that men do lives after them,
The good is oft interred with their bones,

And so it goes.

Not a bad system, all things considered, but of course there are far better systems available today. Keep in mind, however, that all systems are in a sense "Loci Systems," since we have to associate that which we hope to recall with something else, a cue or reminder.

The Body File is such a system.

The Body File

In the Body File System, we associate ten items with ten places (locations) on our own bodies.

The first location, or number one, is going to be our toes, at the very bottom of our bodies, moving up, the second location will be our knees, number three will be the powerful muscles in our upper legs, and number four will be our rear end. Number five will be our lungs and number six will be our shoulders. Moving up further, number seven will be our collar, and number eight will be our face, number nine will be our brain, and finally, number ten will be our scalp.

So we move from our toes up to our scalp. Again, number one will be our toes, number two will be our knees, number three will be the muscles in our upper legs, number four our rear end, number five our lungs, number six our shoulders, number seven our collar, number eight our face, number nine: our brain and finally, number ten our scalp.

Please take a few moments to memorize the body file as it appears on the following page before we move on.

THE BODY FILE

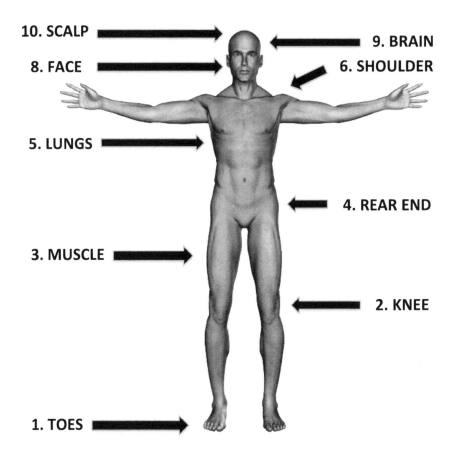

10. SCALP

9. BRAIN

8. FACE

6. SHOULDER

5. LUNGS

4. REAR END

3. MUSCLE

2. KNEE

1. TOES

Now let's apply our body file to the following grocery list that appears on the next page:

The Grocery List

1. **Cereal**
2. **Waffles**
3. **Sugar**
4. **Watermelon**
5. **Cookies**
6. **Oranges**
7. **Ketchup**
8. **Butter**
9. **Vitamins**
10. **Pizza**

The first item we hope to get is cereal, number two is waffles, number three is sugar, four watermelon, five cookies, six oranges, seven ketchup, eight butter. Number nine is vitamins and finally, number ten is pizza.

We've just learned that the number one in our body file is toes. What we hope to do here is to associate toes with cereal. How might you do that? Well, you might see someone holding a spoon between his or her toes and actually eating cereal out of a bowl. See yourself sitting at the breakfast table not eating off the breakfast table, but, rather, see yourself cupping the bowl in your left hand and using your right foot with the spoon between your toes to scoop up the cereal. Please take a moment to see that image in your mind.

Next, we are going to make an association between waffles and the word in our body file that represents the number two - knee. Well, if you were to kneel on a waffle for some time it would make a waffle impression on your knees. See yourself kneeling on two stale waffles. When you stand up, you've got the imprint of the waffle on your knees, see this image in your mind's eye before we go on.

Number three in our grocery list is sugar and our body part is muscle, specifically the large muscle in your thigh. It would take a great deal of muscle to lift a fifty-pound bag of sugar and throw it over your shoulder, see yourself lifting, with your legs, this fifty-pound bag of sugar. Please take a moment to see that image in your mind.

Number four in our grocery list is watermelon, and the body file name for the number four is rear end. How might you make that association? Perhaps as you drop down into your office chair, you crush a watermelon that someone had sat there, and it goes all over your desk and clothing and the floor. Please take a moment to see that image in your mind.

Number five is cookies and lungs represents the number five in our body file. If you were to carelessly inhale while you were stuffing down a cookie, you might end up choking on the cookie crumbs you wave breathed in.

Number six in our body file is shoulders and we have oranges in our grocery list. Why not see yourself with an orange being balanced on each of your two shoulders, and you're walking, trying to make sure that they don't fall off. Picture the two oranges on each of your shoulders.

Please take a moment to see that image in your mind.

Number seven is ketchup, and collar represented the number seven in our body file. Think of your partner coming home with ketchup, not lipstick, on their collar.. They've been two-timing you with Ronald McDonald, please take a moment to see that image in your mind.

Number eight: butter and in our body file, the number eight was represented by face.

Well, perhaps you've run out of face cream, so as you prepare for bed at night, rather than putting face cream on your face, you rub in half a pound of butter on your face Please take a moment to see that image.

Number nine: vitamins. In our body file we said number nine was represented by brain. There is some evidence, not terribly compelling, that vitamins improve our cognitive abilities, or our brain power. Make that association, see yourself taking vitamins every day, maybe by the handful, to improve your intelligence or brain power. See that image in your mind.

Finally, pizza for number ten.. In the body file, the number ten is represented by scalp. See yourself taking home that frozen pizza from the supermarket, but rather than carrying it out in a bag, you're balancing it on your head, it's resting on top of your scalp. Please take a moment to see that image in your mind.

Let's now turn the page now and see if you can remember you grocery list.

The Grocery List

1. _____

2. _____

3. _____

4. _____

5. _____

6. _____

7. _____

8. _____

9. _____

10. _____

How did you do, were you able to get all ten, more importantly, do you now recognize the role intervening variables (in this case, body parts) plays in assisting recall?

The Office File

Another useful system that I would recommend you adopt is the Office File system. It is a simple loci system that can be easily learned and can act like mental "sticky notes."

Think of yourself entering your office in the morning and you look around this important piece of your environment.
The first thing you see, as you come through the **door**, you see the center of you business world - your **desk** and behind it you have a **chair**. On your desktop you have a **computer** and attached to your computer is a **mouse**. You also see on your desktop a **stapler** and a **pen** and a **letter opener**. On the wall you hangs a **clock** next to the **window**.

What we have just created is a simple loci system built around your world. You can of course do the same thing with your home. Rather than memorize these locations sit at your desk, look around and create your own. You don't need more than ten. This is a quick and dirty system for simply applications only.

1. **Door**
2. **Desk**
3. **Chair**
4. **Computer**
5. **Mouse**
6. **Stapler**
7. **Pen**
8. **Letter Opener**
9. **Clock**
10. **Window**

The problem however, with both the loci method and the body list is that there are clear limits to how far you can actually go. We need an intuitive system without limits that can lend itself readily to a myriad of applications. The modified peg system is just such a system; this is a very powerful system, and a very useful system with many practical applications.

Chapter Three

The Peg System

We can call 17th century French mathematician Pierre Hérigone the father of the peg system although his work was further broadened and expanded by Stanislaus Mink von Wennsshein and Henry Herdson around the same time.

The idea behind their systems was essentially to assign an image or object to a number in a sense to give personality to each one..

In 1879 an Englishman named John Sambrook created a rhyming system of visual pegs.

Rhyming Pegs

1 = sun

2 = shoe

3 = tree

4 = door

5 = hive

6 = sticks

7 = heaven

8 = gate

9 = vine

10 = hen

The idea behind this system was ingeniously simple yet effective. If a person were to memorize the rhyming pegs, a simple task, then associate these pegs with the respective items in a list, they could be more readily recalled.

For example if I wanted to remember the first item on my shopping list was butter, I might see in my mind a pad of butter melting having been left outside in the bright sun. If the second item on my list was bananas, I might see a banana in my shoe. To remember my third item eggs I visual a tree with eggs rather than leaves, etc.

This system works fine however it is very limited. What do you rhyme with 17 or 86 or 439?

It was one hundred years later that an English scientist named Richard Grey came up with an important modification by replacing the rhyming words with consonants. His original system looked like this:

b	d	t	f	l	s	p	k	n	z
1	2	3	4	5	6	7	8	9	0

This, except for the rearrangement of the consonants, is the system we use today and describe here.

The Peg System is based on phonetics and the fact that, as Richard Grey noted, in the English language, there are basically ten consonant sounds, if you ignore a, e, i, o, u, and maybe the y sound, you're left with basically ten consonant sounds in our language.

Now, of course here in the West, we're on the base 10 numbering system. Base 10 is the system we use in most of the modern world, This is not the only numbering system; the Babylonians used base 60, the Maya base 20, but in base 10 we have only one to nine plus zero. That's all we have and every other number is a combination of these ten digits.

Since these two things coincide, ten places in our numbering system, ten consonant sounds in our language, why don't we arbitrarily assign one of these consonant sounds to each of the digits.

You may want, at this point, to refer to the consonant provided below:

1	**T, D**
2	**N**
3	**M**
4	**R**
5	**L**
6	**Sh, Ch, J**
7	**K, C**
8	**F, V**
9	**B, P**
0	**Z, S**

In our system, the number one will always be represented by the sound made by the letters T or D. It is actually not those letters but the sound that they make.

When you pronounce the sound represented by the letter T (tuh), or D (duh), your tongue is in the same relationship to your teeth and to your palate. The sound is essentially the same; it is this unique consonant sound that will, by our rules, always represent the number one.

The number two will always be represented by the sound made by the letter N. Again remember it is the sound the letter N makes, not the letter itself, the sound the letter N makes in the words NO or NOT or NOAH.

The number three will be represented by the M sound, as in the words MA or MAKE or MOTHER.

The R sound in our system will always represent the number four, as in ROW or RYE.

The L sound represents the number five, as in LOW or LAW or LAWYER.

The hard C sound made by the SH or the CH or J will represent the number six. This sound is SH as in SHOULD or the CH as in CHEESE.

The K or C sounds will represent the number seven. The K sound as in KEY, or as in KITE, or as in COW.

The number eight will always be represented by the sound made by the letters F or V. The F sound as in FEE or the V sound as in IVY.

The B or the P sounds will represent the number nine.

Finally, the Z or S sounds will represent the number zero. The sound made by the Z in the word ZOO or the S sound as in the word SNAKE.

At this point you might be thinking, this is immensely complex, not only are you required to remember the geometric shapes that we call numbers, but now I have to remember *sh, kuh, ch* – sounds!

Well, if we left it there, it wouldn't help you at all.

But we're not going to leave it there, we're going to take it one step further, and in so doing, we're going to come up with a very simple yet a very workable system.

We said that vowels don't represent numbers, nor do they, but in conjunction with consonants, vowels enable us to create words; and words that we'll choose will represent only the numbers that we're interested in.

We're going to call these peg words, and there's going to be a peg word for every number.

But before we introduce you to the Peg System, please take a few minutes to commit the Peg Words to memory. This will help you adopt the Peg System with greater ease and will facilitate its implementation.

Two aids that might help you do this. First, to help you remember that the number one is represented by the letters "T" or "D," recognize that there is just one down stroke in the letters "T" or "D." To learn that the letter "N represents the number two" remember there are two down strokes in the letter "N." Think of the 3M Corporation to bring those two together. The letter "R" represents the number four. The last letter in the number four is the letter R. The letter "L" represent the number five. If you hold your left hand out in front of you, your index finger and thumb form an "L." Also the Roman numeral for 50 is "L." The number six is represented by the letters "Sh," "Ch" or "J" (essentially the same sound). A reversed "J" looks somewhat similar to the number six. The letters "K" or "C" represent the number seven. The number "7" tilted to the left looks a little like a skeleton KEY and two "7's" can form a lowercase "K." The number eight is represented by the number "F" or "V". A lowercase cursive "F" and "8" both have both have two loops. Think of a V-8 engine. The number nine is represented by the "B" or "P." The mirror image of "9" resembles an uppercase "P." Finally, the letters "Z" or "S" represent the number zero. The first letter in the word zero is a "Z."

Second, if you recall the Body file system we introduced you to in the last chapter you may recognize that the ten body parts begin with the same letters as the Phonetic Pegs.

The Phonetic Code

1	Toes	T, D
2	Knee	N
3	Muscle	M
4	Rear End	R
5	Lungs	L
6	Shoulder	Sh, Ch, J
7	Collar	K, C
8	Face	F, V
9	Brain	B, P
0	Scalp	Z, S

When you feel you have committed the phonetic code to memory, please turn the page and complete exercises 3.1 and 3.2 before moving forward with the program.

Practice Exercise 3.1
The Phonetic Code

For each of the following numbers enter the corresponding phonetic sound in the space provided:

1. _____   3. _____   7. _____

9. _____   8. _____   2. _____

4. _____   5. _____   6. _____

Practice Exercise 3.2
The Phonetic Code

For each of the following phonetic sounds enter the corresponding number in the space provided:

N _____   Sh _____   K _____

R _____   T _____   F _____

Z _____   L _____   M _____

D _____   S _____   C _____

These "Peg Words" for the numbers one through nine plus zero are shown below. It should be noted that the choice of these particular words is arbitrary as of course was the assignment of the individual consonants to numbers that we chose above.   Many words would suffice. There are several words that would work equally as well. For example, we could use Tea for number one or Cow for number seven.

The Peg System

1. **Tie**

2. **Noah**

3. **Ma**

4. **Rye**

5. **Law**

6. **Shoe**

7. **Key**

8. **Ivy**

9. **Bee**

0. **Zoo**

The number one will be represented by a word that contains only the t or the d consonant sound; it can have any number of vowels; because they exist only to create words. As you can see, the word I have chosen is the word "tie." It is important that we choose, where possible, a concrete noun, this is because we want to visualize the peg word quickly and associate it with the item we hope to recall.

The word TIE will work well, it is a concrete noun and contains only one consonant sound – the T sound that represents the number one.

The "ie" in the word TIE doesn't represent anything, these letters, the vowel sound they represent simply create the word.

You can readily see a tie in your mind's eye, and you can associate a tie with something else. In a moment I'll show you how.

For the number two, we need a word that contains only the N consonant sound, it can have any number of vowels, but it can only have the one consonant N which represents the number two.

Now, the obvious choice and the simplest word would be the word NO.

But as you can see, I haven't chosen the word NO; rather, I've chosen the word NOAH. Why? Because it's a better mental picture, it's harder to see NO in your mind than it is to see the prophet Noah.

Most of us have some experience with the Bible story of Noah and Noah's Ark and the animals two by two. When I see Noah, there's a mental picture there already; that's why I've chosen it, Noah still follows the rules, it's a word that contains one consonant sound followed by two vowels: O and AH. These vowels do not assist our recall, they complete the word. Again it's only the consonants that represent numbers, so Noah could represent the number two.

Your mother, or your MA, could represent the number three, in the word MA, you have one consonant sound: the M sound followed by AH, a vowel sound.

By the same line of reasoning RYE could represent the number four. The only consonant sound in the word RYE is the R, we can visualize loaf of rye bread, a bottle of rye whiskey.

The number five is LAW. You might visualize a policeman, a policewoman, a set of scales, a Mountie, a judge sitting at his or her bench or an attorney, any of those images and several more would suffice.

The number six is SHOE, the number seven is KEY, the number eight is IVY. In the case of IVY the consonant is sandwiched between two vowels – I and E. Number nine is BEE and zero is represented by the word Zoo.

Now we have a word, or more importantly, an image for the numbers one through nine plus zero. If we commit this list to our memory once we can use it over and over to remember items in a list.

It is called the peg system because, speaking metaphorically if we have a series of peg words committed to memory, we have a series of pegs on which we can hang the information or facts we wish to recall simply through the use of our imagination.

On the next page we will show how this knowledge or "system" can be used to remember a simple grocery list.

The Grocery List

1. Chicken

2. Watermelons

3. Flour

4. Coffee

5. Newspaper

6. Cherries

7. Sardines

8. Apples

9. Peanut Butter

Our first item is CHICKEN and our peg word for number one is, of course, TIE. What we need to do is absurdly associate the two. One way we might do this is to see a barnyard full of chickens all wearing neckties. As we discussed previously we have to make the mental picture stand out by drawing on the right side of our brain.

Take a moment to see this picture in your mind. It is important that you actually see the picture in your mind's eye. It is not how long you see it; it's the clarity of the image.

Next, we wish to associate NOAH, our Peg Word for number two and WATERMELONS. We might view Noah standing on the deck of his ark. But he does not have any animals on board, just watermelons! See watermelons rolling up the ramp two by two in your mind's eye.

Number three is FLOUR and our Peg Word is MA. See your mother covered in flour, as if someone poured a 50 lb. bag of flour over her.

The Peg Word for number four is RYE and we want to associate RYE with COFFEE. See yourself poring a generous portion of rye whiskey into you coffee, every time you have a cup of coffee throughout the day.

Next we want to associate the fifth item in our list NEWSPAPER with your symbol for LAW. Perhaps you might see the judge at his bench, ignoring the pleas from the attorneys as he reads his newspaper. Or, maybe you see a policeman or a policewoman reading a newspaper oblivious to the robberies, assaults and mayhem taking place just outside your squad car.

The sixth item in our list is Cherries and our Peg Word is SHOE. As you slip your foot into your favorite shoe you hear a squishing sound and feel moisture on your toes. Someone has put a few juicy cherries in your shoes. Take a moment to see that image before we go on.

Item number seven is SARDINES. The Peg Word is KEY. Perhaps you are trying to open the tin of sardines with a key and you're having difficulty and you're lacerating your fingers. See this troubling picture in your mind's eye.

The eighth item in our grocery list is APPLES and our Peg Word is IVY. Picture an ivy covered building you know, but every place where a leaf should be there is an apple.

The ninth item on our list is PEANUT BUTTER and the ninth Page Word is BEE, the insect. Perhaps you see a large bumblebee flying into your open jar of peanut butter and as it crawls out of the jar and across your counter it leaves a trail of peanut butter. Take a moment to see this last image in your mind, and then turn the page to test your recall.

The Grocery List

1. _____

2. _____

3. _____

4. _____

5. _____

6. _____

7. _____

8. _____

9. _____

Did you find you had little difficulty recalling the list?

You might say that this is fine for one to nine but what about the numbers beyond nine, like 12 or 43 or 674? Does the system breakdown?

No, this is the beauty of the Peg System. There is not limit whatever. What we do with double or triple digit numbers is simply combine respectively the two or three phonetic sounds into one word.

For example for the number ten, we need a Peg Word that might start with the letter T and also contains the Z or S, the sound for zero. TOES would fit the bill as would DICE.

The number 11 could be represented by a word that has the T sound repeated such as TOT.

The Number 12 by TIN, 13 by TIME, 14 by TIRE and so on. A list of the first twenty-five Peg Words is provided below and the pegs for one through one hundred can be found in Appendix A on page xxx.

The Peg Words
(1 through 20)

1. Tie	11. Tot
2. Noah	12. Tin
3. Ma	13. Time
4. Rye	14. Tire
5. Law	15. Tail
6. Shoe	16. Dish
7. Key	17. Tack
8. Ivy	18. T.V.
9. Bee	19. Tub
10. Toes	20. Nose

The question I often get is, "If I use the peg system to remember one list will it not interfere with my ability to remember another?" The short answer is no. As long as there is either an interval of time between the two applications or a difference in the nature of the two lists, there will not be a problem.

To demonstrate this and to provide practice in the system I would ask you to work through the following list with me.

In practice exercise 3.3 on the next few pages, we will memorize the first half of the forty-four men that have served in the Office of President of the United States as of the date of this publication.

We will focus on the last name only. We will demonstrate later in the program how to remember first names.

Mnemonic devices take practice. A theoretical understanding will not help you. You *need* to take the time to work through the practice exercises.

Practice Exercise 3.3
United States Presidents

1. George Washington

Now we all know that George Washington was the first president, nevertheless lets apply our system to all the presidents.

The first rule of the Peg System is that you have to have to replace the idea, information or thing that we wish to remember with some pictorial equivalent. We must establish a visual representation of, in this case, Washington.
I choose the Washington Monument. If you have ever visited Washington, DC you have probably seen this obelisk; it's hard to avoid it. It's 555 feet tall and located at the center or the city.

Our Peg Word for the number one is TIE. Why not visualize a 100-foot necktie tied around the Washington Monument. Perhaps it's a yellow tie to honor the troops.

It is important for you to actually see this visual image in your mind's eye. Don't just read what is written here – see it!

2. John Adams

The second president was John Adams. Again the first thing we will do is to choose a pictorial equivalent, which is a visual image for Adams. You might think of the biblical Adam or atoms or maybe one of the characters in the Addams Family. Maybe you think of Adam's apple or Stacy Adams shoes. All of these will work.

The peg word for number two is Noah. Our challenge now is to come up with a visual association between Noah and one of these substitutes.

When I use the peg word Noah for number two, I always see Noah standing on the deck of his ark as whatever I hope to recall is stacked up on the deck or rolling up the long ramp onto the ark.

In this case, I would see a thousand clones of Adam and Eve holding hands and walking up the ramp.

Remember when we exaggerate the number, 1000's of Adams & Eves.

3. Thomas Jefferson

The third President is Thomas Jefferson. Again we begin by trying to come up with a pictorial equivalent for the word Jefferson.

This could be something from your experience, and failing that it might be something that sounds like the word Jefferson. When I think of Jefferson the first thing that pops into my mind is the old television program "The Jeffersons."

I can see George Jefferson and his wife Wheezy. I might associate then one of those characters with my mother or my MA; the peg word for number three. Maybe she is on the program or maybe she is marrying George.

I could also choose the 60's band, Jefferson Airplane. I might see my mom on the road with the band. She has become a "Roadie" for the band.

4. James Madison

The fourth president was James Madison. A possible substitute is Madison Square Garden or Madison Avenue, the famous advertising street in New York City.

The peg word for number four is "rye." I would see myself attending a fight at Madison Square Garden, but there is a very rowdy crowd tonight and they are throwing their rye whiskey bottles at the fighters.

Take a moment to see this image in your mind's eye.

5. James Monroe

The fourth president is James Monroe. Most people will think of the actress Marilyn Monroe. As a general rule when we choose an image for a name shared by a famous person it is usually best to use that famous person as your visual substitute.

Also it is always best to use the first thing that comes to mind. Why? Because this will be the first thing that will come to mind the next time you seek to recall it.

The peg word for the number five is law. You may recall when we spoke earlier about choosing peg words I said that you could choose your own image to represent that peg word. For example, here we might visualize law by seeing a judge at his bench, or our image might be an attorney, a policeman or policewomen, a set of scales or a Mountie. All of these images are fine, the important thing to remember however is that we should *always* use the same symbol. Don't use a judge one time and a policeman the next. Because if you do so you will slow yourself down by having to also remember what image you had chosen.

No, if you choose to use a Mountie as your image for "law" always use a Mountie. If you choose to use a policeman always use a policeman.

My symbol, the image that always comes to my mind when I think of law, is a judge at his bench. So I might see Marilyn as the judge. Maybe she is dressed like a British high court justice, with the wig and robes.

You might choose the symbol for blind justice, being a blindfolded woman holding a set of scales. This statue is often found on the roof of our courthouses. In this case you would see Marilyn as the woman in the wispy gown holding the scale.

6. John Quincy Adams

Number six is the son of John Adams the second president, John Quincy Adams. We can use the same symbols for Adams that we used with John Adams or a different substitute, either way it will not cause any confusion.

The peg word for number six is "shoe."

I would see Adam and Eve standing in the Garden of Eden, wearing nothing but their shoes. It's the only part of the costume they have figured out. Is that a visual picture?

7. Andrew Jackson

The seventh president was Andrew Jackson. In this case we have to come up with a substitute for the word Jackson. Many people when they hear the word Jackson think of Michael Jackson the pop singer.

The peg word is "key."

I would see little Michael Jackson moonwalking around the stage with a great big heavy gold chain around his neck. And as he dances this key is swinging around hitting him on the back of the head and weighing him down.

That's an absurd picture. See that image in your mind or choose some other substitute for Jackson before we move on.

8. Martin Van Buren

The eighth precedent is Martin Van Buren. Now for the first time we come upon a name that doesn't ring any chimes for most people.

We have all had some exposure to the name Monroe or Jefferson or Jackson but Van Buren is much more obscure.

This is good because it gives us an opportunity practice a technique that we will come back to when I show you how to remember the names of the people we meet in our daily lives.

In situations like this, we choose a phonetic substitute. Something that sounds like it, that is close enough to remind us of the real name.

With Van Buren I would see a van of blue. And what is the van of blue packed full of? Ivy. So much so that if I were to open one of the cargo doors or roll down a window it would fly out in my face. Take a moment to visualize that before we move forward.

9. William Henry Harrison

Our ninth president is William Henry Harrison. What do you think of when you hear the word Harrison? Many people think of the famous actor Harrison Ford and that will work well.

In "Raiders of the Lost Ark," someone or something was always chasing Ford. At one point he was trying to outrun a stone ball rolling down a narrow corridor.

Since our peg word is "bee" I would see Harrison Ford being chased by a huge swarm of killer bees, life sized bees.

10. John Tyler

John Tyler is the tenth president. Originally our surnames came from where we lived or what we did for a living. Taylor was someone who sewed, Cooper made barrels and so on. Tyler originally denoted someone who tiled cathedrals or laid down cobblestone. In our day this would be a tradesperson who might tile your bathroom or kitchen.

I found myself occasionally with people who were grievously injured in battle; men who had lost limbs. Yet in many cases these people overcame these disabilities and did remarkable things. Like the person who learns to hold a paintbrush between their toes and create beautiful intricate paintings.

Well in the case of John Tyler, here we have someone so proficient that they can actually tile your bathroom with their toes. He can hold a trowel between his toes. See that mental picture before you read on.

11. James K. Polk

Our 11th president's name is James Polk. Our peg word is "tot."

I would see myself stepping into an elevator only to be poked by a horrible little kid with a pointed stick. He is poking everyone.

12. Zachary Taylor

The 12th president was Zachary Taylor. We could choose the tailor, that is, someone who sews or weaves, or I might choose as my substitute a famous person with that same name such as Elizabeth Taylor. If I chose the craft of tailoring I might see myself trying to put on a pair of trousers woven of tin.

If I chose to use the image of Elizabeth Taylor the actress as my substitute, I would see all that platinum jewelry that her ex-husbands' had given her that she thought was platinum turning out to be tin. Her fingers have black residue on them.

13. Millard Fillmore.

The 13th president was Millard Fillmore. The word Fillmore is easy because it represents an action. I can see myself "filling more" liquid into a container. Maybe more gasoline into my car, more milk into my cereal. Our peg word for number thirteen is time. Well it would certainly take more time to fill more gas into a Hummer than it would a Toyota Camry. See yourself filling more liquid into some container before we go to number fifteen.

14. Franklin Pierce

Franklin Pierce was our 14th president. In this instance we might want to go with the verb pierce. Our peg word is "tire," Perhaps you might see yourself piercing your boss's tires.

15. James Buchanan

Our 15th president was James Buchanan. The peg word for number fifteen is "tail." There is a conservative commentator that still pops up on CNN, Fox and MSNBC by the name of Pat Buchanan but his name is not really a household word. I would use the substitute cannon, which as you will see is really close enough.

The wick coming out of the canon looks something like a tail. I might visualize it as a tail – a striped tiger's tail, and when you light it you hear a yelping sound.

16. Abraham Lincoln

Our 16th president was Abraham Lincoln. In this case we may not even need a substitute because we already have a pretty good image of the man in our minds.

Most pictures of Abraham Lincoln show him dressed in a black suit and wearing a stovepipe hat. Since our peg word is dish, why not see a little satellite dish on top of his hat, now that's pretty absurd. Some people say, well why not go with a Lincoln town car or limo that's more realistic. Well they have answered their own question; it is more realistic. We don't want realistic. We want *absurd*, so take a moment to see Abe walking around with a small satellite dish on top of his top hat.

17. Andrew Johnson

Andrew Johnson is number seventeen. Substitutes might include Johnson & Johnson products, or Johnson wax.

Our peg word is "tack." If you were to lay down Johnson wax on your kitchen floor only to walk on it before it was completely dry it's going to be a little bit tacky.

18. Ulysses S. Grant

Our 18th president is Ulysses S. Grant. Well again we could go with a substitute of a famous person of the same name Amy Grant, or Hugh Grant. We could, of course, see ourselves as being the recipient of a huge grant.

Our peg word is, "TV" or television. I might see myself settling in for a quiet night of television watching only to find all the television channels are playing Hugh Grant pictures back-to-back 24/7, it's a Hugh Grantapolusa.

19. Rutherford Hayes

Our 19th president was Rutherford Hayes. Well Hayes, is easy with hay being the substitute. The peg word is "tub."

You have just checked into a hotel room and would like to take a bath but notice that there is hay in the tub, obviously the last occupant of the room was a horse. Form that association before we move on.

20. Charles Garfield

Charles Garfield was our 20th president. Obviously the substitute is that famous cat Garfield. Our peg word is "nose."

Well if you are holding that big old cat and a dog comes by that it is not familiar with its claws will come out and it will grab hold. I might see Garfield grabbing on to my nose with his claws as the dog barks up at him and as he spins around he tears my nose up.

21. Chester Arthur

Our twenty-first present was Chester Arthur and our peg word is "nut."

When I think of Arthur, I think of the character Dudley Moore played in the film "Arthur." What a nut!

22. Grover Cleveland

President number twenty-two was Grover Cleveland. The page word for twenty-two is "nun."

If you are able to remember Sesame Street you will recollect Grover that little blue puppet with the big red nose. Let's dress him up in a nun's habit. That is certainly absurd and perhaps a little troubling. But see it in your mind' eye.

Well that is the first half of the forty-four presidents. Take a few moments to go back and review one last time and then try your best enter the presidents last name below:

The Presidents

1. _____   12. _____

2. _____   13. _____

3. _____   14. _____

4. _____   15. _____

5. _____   16. _____

6. _____   17. _____

7. _____   18. _____

8. _____   19. _____

9. _____   20. _____

10. _____   21. _____

11. _____   22. _____

Practice Session 3.2

Following the same pattern we established with the first twenty-two presidents, practice the technique on the remaining twenty-two. It is not necessary for you to memorize the peg words for 23 through 44. They are provided below for your convenience. The point of this exercise is to practice your visual associations only.

My experience in having worked with the peg system for over thirty years is that twenty-five pegs are enough. You will see in the next chapter that there are better systems we can utilize when dealing with large numbers.

US Presidents
The Next Twenty-Two

23. Benjamin Harrison (Gnome)

24. Grover Cleveland (Nero)

25. William McKinley (Nail)

26. Theodore Roosevelt (Wench)

27. William Howard Taft (Neck)

28. Woodrow Wilson (Knife)

29. Warren G. Harding (Knob)

30. Calvin Coolidge (Mouse)

31. Herbert Hoover (Maid)

32. Franklin Roosevelt (Money)

33. Harry S. Truman (Mummy)

34. Dwight D. Eisenhower (Mower)

35. John F. Kennedy (Mule)

36. Lyndon B. Johnson (Match)

37. Richard Nixon (Hammock)

38. Gerald Ford (Mafia)

39. Jimmy Carter (Mop)

40. Ronald Reagan (Rose)

41. George H. Bush (Radio)

42. Bill Clinton (Horn)

43. George W. Bush (Army)

44. Barack Obama (Warrior)

When you are ready, turn the page and enter the names of each of the last twenty-two presidents:

The US Presidents
(23 through 44)

23. _____

24. _____

25. _____

26. _____

27. _____

28. _____

29. _____

30. _____

31. _____

32. _____

33. _____

34. _____

35. _____

36. _____

37. _____

38. _____

39. _____

40. _____

41. _____

42. _____

43. _____

44. _____

Practice Session 3.4

The following guided exercise will provide further practice in the use of the peg system. There are a few suggestions should you need further assistance.

The Canadian Prime-Ministers

1. Sir John A. Macdonald
2. Alexander Mackenzie
3. Sir John J. C. Abbott
4. Sir John S. D. Thompson
5. Sir Mackenzie Bowell
6. Sir Charles Tupper
7. Sir Wilfred Laurier
8. Sir Robert L. Borden
9. Arthur Meighen
10. W. L. M. King
11. Richard B. Bennett
12. Louis St. Laurent
13. John Diefenbaker
14. Lester B. Pearson
15. Pierre E. Trudeau
16. Joseph Clark
17. John Turner
18. Brian Mulroney
19. Kim Campbell
20. Jean Chrétien
21. Paul Martin
22. Stephen Harper

Practice Session 3.4

Guided Suggestions

1. John A. Macdonald

The first Canadian prime minister's name was John A. Macdonald, to remember Macdonald; you must come up with a pictorial equivalent for the name Macdonald.

You can do that in one of two ways. This is an important concept for you to grasp because we'll come back to this when we discuss how to remember the names of the people you meet in your daily lives. You can either choose a concrete image from your own experience for the same word, or you can choose a mental image of something, which is phonetically close to the word we are trying to recall.

Macdonald, can you think of anything concrete that has that name, what comes to mind when you hear that word?

For many people, the word Macdonald suggests the fast-food restaurant - McDonald's. There are many good symbols there that might work: the golden arches, Ronald McDonald, the Big Mac, any of those symbols could represent the word Macdonald.

Let's choose the golden arches.

The peg word for number one is "tie." You want to bring those two words together in a way that absurdly associates one with the other, you might think of the golden arches with a necktie tied around them in a large bow, that's a good mental picture, that draws on the right side of the brain, it's visual and absurd.

2. Alexander Mackenzie

The second Canadian prime minister's name was Alexander Mackenzie. We will associate that name with our peg word for number two, "Noah."

Does the word Mackenzie mean anything to you? If you are Canadian, you might know that the longest river in Canada is the Mackenzie River, it's often referred to as the Mighty Mackenzie. What then might you see coming down the Mighty Mackenzie? Noah's Ark.

3. John Abbott

The third prime minister's name was John Abbott. For many of us, the word Abbott suggests the comedy team of Abbott and Costello. Who will you associate Abbott and Costello with? Your "ma," the peg word for number three.

How might you do that, well, maybe your mother is marrying one of them or perhaps she is engaged in one of the comedy team's slapstick skits, or maybe your mother has moved to the Abby and taken on the role of Mother Abbess. Can you see your mother lost in these dark robes?

4. John Thompson

The fourth prime minister's name was Thompson, and we want to associate some representation of Thompson and our peg word for number four which is "rye."

What substitute might you come up with for the word Thompson? Tom Thumb, the Thompson machine gun?

Little Tom Thumb, where can he sleep at night? In a rye bottle, make that association before we go on to number five.

5. McKenzie Bowell

The peg word for five is law and again, your image for law may be a judge, a set of scales, a cop, it really doesn't matter. What does matter is that each time you use this system you're consistent. Don't use a judge one time and an attorney the next and a policeman the next time.

The name is Bowell, maybe his honor isn't sitting on the bench today. – he is sitting somewhere else! Make your own association between Bowell and your symbol for law, it shouldn't be very difficult, use your own imagination.

6. Charles Tupper

Our peg word is "shoe." The prime minister's name was Charles Tupper.

What first comes to mind when you hear the word Tupper? Many people think of Tupperware. Tupperware what? Tupperware shoes. Maybe you've got a closet full of these translucent plastic shoes and when you walk in them, they burp. See that in your mind's eye.

7. Wilfred Laurier

The seventh Canadian prime minister's name is Wilfred Laurier. What do you think of when you hear the word, Laurier? In Ottawa, the national's capital, there's a great hotel called Château Laurier.

Perhaps when you register at the Château Laurier, the "key" they give you is enormous, and you must walk down Sparks or Wellington with it over your shoulder.

What else, well, what do they call a truck in England? They call it a lorry. See a little British lorry with a great huge key sticking out of the back of it.

You have to wind it up before you can drive it through the streets of London.

8. Robert Borden

The peg word for number eight is "ivy," and the name of the eighth prime minister is Robert Borden. What do you think of when you hear the word Borden? Perhaps, Borden milk products, Camp Borden or Lizzie Borden. Maybe we see Lizzie taking her axe and giving the ivy forty whacks.

9. Arthur Meighen

The ninth prime minister was Arthur Meighen and peg word for number nine is the insect "bee." For many of us, the word Meighen doesn't ring any bells, but that's good because it gives us an opportunity to practice the second technique in remembering names, choosing a phonetic substitute.

Is there anything you could picture that sounds like Meighen and that is close enough to remind you of it? The word "mean" is close and would work. See yourself being chased down the street by a huge, mean killer bee.

You may wish to continue through the remainder of list:

1. Sir John A. Macdonald
2. Alexander Mackenzie
3. Sir John J. C. Abbott
4. Sir John S. D. Thompson
5. Sir Mackenzie Bowell
6. Sir Charles Tupper
7. Sir Wilfred Laurier
8. Sir Robert L. Borden
9. Arthur Meighen
10. W. L. M. King
12. Louis St. Laurent
13. John Diefenbaker
14. Lester B. Pearson
15. Pierre E. Trudeau
16. Joseph Clark
17. John Turner
18. Brian Mulroney
19. Kim Campbell
20. Jean Chrétien
21. Paul Martin

The Canadian Prime-Ministers

1. _____

2. _____

3. _____

4. _____

5. _____

6. _____

7. _____

8. _____

9. _____

10. _____

11. _____

12. _____

13. _____

14. _____

15. _____

16. _____

17. _____

18. _____

19. _____

20. _____

21. _____

22. _____

Chapter Four

Remembering Numbers

The peg system is very useful for remembering lists and other forms of sequential information but can it be used to assist us in remembering longer numbers, for example dates in history or telephone numbers?

The answer is yes and no.

It would take a great deal of time to memorize all the four digit numbers and probably the rest of our lives to memorize all seven-digit numbers. In this respect the peg system will not assist us here. The phonetic code however, on which the peg system is predicated, can aid us greatly in remembering numbers.

Have a look at the twelve-digit number below, how could you apply the information that you learned in the peg system to remember this number?

4-1-1-5-3-7-5-2-6-4-1-6

Remember that we said each of the peg words was based on a phonetic code, we chose tie for number one because it contained within it the consonant sound for number one, the sound made when we say "T" or "D." For number two, the consonant sound was "N" three "M" and so on.

In order to recall this particular number (perhaps it's a calling card number or a credit number), the first step is to convert each of the digits contained within that number to their corresponding phonetic equivalent.

Four is the "R" sound and one is the "T" sound. We have that number and sound repeated, so we now have R-T-T Five is the "L" sound; three is the "M" sound; seven the "K" sound; five again the "L" sound; two the "N;" six is the "Sh;" four the "R;" one the "T;" and six, again, is the "Sh" sound, with this conversion we now have:

4-1-1-5-3-7-5-2-6-4-1-6

R-T-T-L-M-K-L-N-Ch-R-T-Sh

Next we break this number into chunks. 4-1-1-5, although we could start with 4-1-1 or 4-1-1-5-3. You will learn with practice how many digit you work best with.

Four consonant sounds now have replaced the digits 4-1-1-5:

R T T L

Now by simply adding a vowel or two we can create a word.

R a T T L e

R A T T L E

Rattle can *only* represent 4-1-1-5. So what we have done is replace a four digit number with a word.

Going on, the three we said was the "M" sound, and seven was the "K." Can you think of a word containing just the "M" and the "K" consonant sounds? Remember too in your selection to choose, where possible, a concrete noun or at least an active verb.

Mike or *Mack* would work.

3   7

M   K

MacK

Five is the "L" sound, two is the "N," six the "Sh," and four is "R." By throwing a couple of vowels in, we could have *launcher* or *launcher* or *lawn chair*.

5   2   6   4

L   N   Sh   R

LawNCHaiR

LAWNCHAIR

Finally, sixteen is "T" and "Sh." Why not use the peg word for number 16, which we have already memorized.

1 6

D Sh

Dish

So we've broken this twelve-digit number down into four words: *Rattle, Mack, Lawn chair, and Dish.*

All that is left is to form a simple chain as we did with the former list you learned   Trees-Airplaine-Envelope-Nuns-Motorcycle-Supermarket-Fire-Teapot-Mouse-Book.

You might think of a rattle on the hood of the Mack truck, if you recall, the Mack is the a large truck that has a bulldog as a hood ornament. We are going to replace the bulldog with a rattle.

After Mack is lawn chair, see the Mack truck running over your beautiful new lawn chair and smashing that very expensive china dish that you had placed on the arm.

See the story in my mind's eye: Rattle replaces hood ornament on Mack, Mack runs over the lawn chair, smashes dish.

To recall this number then it is just a matter of decoding the story.

RaTTLe MacK LawNChaiR DiSh

4 1 1 5   3 7   5 2 6 4   1 6

This number incidentally, represents the calendar for the year 2009. Each digit in that twelve-digit number represents a different month in the year

2009. The first 4 represents January; the first 1 February; the second 1 March; 5 represents April and so on. The last digit, the twelve number - 6 would represent December.

The value of the number itself represents the first Sunday in each month respectively. So the first 4 tells us, that in the month of January 2009, the first Sunday was the fourth. In February, the first Sunday was the first, likewise the first Sunday in March was also the first. In April the first Sunday was the fifth, and in May it was the third. The last number - six representing December indicates that the first Sunday in December was the sixth.

So if you had to recall, off the top of your head, which day of the week Christmas fell on in 2009 by simply adding twenty-one days to six. Six plus twenty-one is twenty-seven. So we know that the twenty-seventh was a Sunday, therefore the 26, Boxing Day was a Saturday and Christmas Day fell on a Friday in 2009.

It can be a very useful thing to be able to identify the day of the week for any date without having to refer to a calendar or organizer.

This principle of replacing numbers with their corresponding consonant sounds and then making words out of them is the way in which we deal with long numbers such as credit or calling card numbers.

I gave you an example from a previous year so you might practice on the current year.

The code for 2010 is:

2-6-6-3-1-5-3-7-4-2-6-4

and 2012 is:

1-5-4-1-6-3-1-5-2-7-4-2

and 2013 is:

6-3-3-7-5-2-7-4-1-6-3-1

Lets take one of these as another example. Let us choose the year 2012 and convert it to its respective consonant sounds:

1-5-4-1-6-3-1-5-2-7-4-2
T-L-L-T-Sh-M-T-L-N-K-R-N

Don't forget as you convert that one can be replaced by "D" as well as "T," and six can be represented by "Ch" as well as "Sh." So we could also have:

D-L-L-D-Ch-M-D-L-N-K-R-N

Next we will attempt to form words around these consonants by adding vowels:

DuLlaRD ShaMeD LoNg RuN

How would I chain these words together? I would simply think of the fact that dullards who do not take the time or make the effort to improve their skills, as you now are, will be shamed in the long run.

Seldom are we required to recall twelve digit numbers, but we are instead required to remember numbers in series. Dates in history or telephone numbers are an example.

Consider the following list of dates in history:

Dates In History

Charles Lindbergh's Flight	1927
The Death of F.D.R	1945
First British Parliament	1295
Death Of Napoleon	1821
Pilgrim's Landing	1620
Lindbergh's Flight	1927
Hitler Becomes Chancellor	1933
Harvard University Est.	1636
Battle Of Waterloo	1815
French Revolution	1789

The first thing I will do as I approach any series is to simplify the task as much as possible by identifying any commonality in the list. In this case, all of the dates shown occurred in the last millennia, that is, all of the dates begin with the number one; therefore we can eliminate the number one from each date, resulting in the following truncated list:

Dates in History

Charles Lindbergh's Flight	927
The Death of F.D.R	945
First British Parliament	295
Death Of Napoleon	821

Pilgrim's Landing	**620**
Lindbergh's Flight	**927**
Hitler Becomes Chancellor	**933**
Harvard University Est.	**636**
Battle Of Waterloo	**815**
French Revolution	**789**

Our next step is to take each date separately and convert it to its consonant equivalent, for example:

Lindbergh's Transatlantic Flight - 927

$$9 \quad 2 \quad 7$$
$$B \quad N \quad K$$

Then adding whatever vowel or vowels necessary, in this case "a," we create a word:

BaN K

Could you associate BANK with Charles Lindbergh's first transatlantic flight? Very easily, see him banking his plane, or flying from bank to bank.

Franklin D. Roosevelt died in 1945. Again, having reduced this to 9-4-5, I then replace each number with its consonant equivalent:

9   4   5
B   R   L
BuRiaL

I might choose BURIAL, which could be easily associated with the event.

The first British parliament occurred in 1295, by the same method I might get:

2   9   5
N   B   L
NoBLe

Presumably all were noblemen at this first parliament.

Lets look at another example. The following is a list of area codes for selected Canadian cities. This is not incidentally meant to be an exhaustive list.

Calgary	**403**
Vancouver	**604**
Toronto	**416**
Winnipeg	**204**
Regina	**306**
Montreal	**514**
Halifax	**902**
Fredericton	**506**
Barrie	**705**
Thunder Bay	**807**
St. John's	**709**

As before, the first thing I would do in approaching this task is look for commonality in the series. Is there anything that this series of numbers have in common? They all have zero as the center digit, except for the two largest cities in Canada, Toronto and Montreal.

This rule allows me to reduce this list then to a series of two digit numbers:

Calgary	**43**
Vancouver	**64**
Toronto	**46**
Winnipeg	**24**
Regina	**36**
Montreal	**54**

Halifax	92
Fredericton	56
Barrie	75
Thunder Bay	87
St. John's	79

Next I choose a word containing just those two consonant sounds, perhaps even a word that is indicative or indigenous to that city.

Calgary   4   3

Calgary   R   M

Calgary   RAM

Calgary has a view of the **R**ocky **M**ountains where **RAM**s live and butt heads.

Vancouver has the area code 604.

Vancouver   6   4

Vancouver   Sh   R

Vancouver   SHORE

Vancouver is on the coast; by the sea**shore,** although anyone who has spent any time there might remember it better by making the association with SHOWER.

The area code for Toronto is 416.

Toronto   4   6

Toronto   R   Sh

Toronto   RadiSH

New York is the "Big Apple," Toronto is the "Big Radish!"

In Section Three of the "Before Test" you were asked to take a few moments to memorize fifteen six-digit numbers and then associated each with a random number. Many people found this to be an impossible feat.

The truth is however, that not only is it not impossible, it is really not that difficult.

At my public seminars, I demonstrate how I am able to memorize a list, like the one below, comprised of 800 random numbers in less than thirty minutes.

Random Numbers

30 - 420121	2 - 111235	35 - 424824	74 - 438190
69 - 314781	68 - 374156	50 - 754932	34 - 634718
25 - 968010	3 - 313471	82 - 390998	81 - 809987
16 - 419217	87 - 605493	36 - 574932	52 - 816730
47 - 850947	21 - 032695	95 - 201123	5 - 187527
91 - 850151	75 - 182022	98 - 780112	93 - 220112
13 - 224606	56 - 061785	62 - 217853	45 - 344594
64 - 370774	49 - 805381	58 - 576392	33 - 424608
89 - 897639	94 - 101123	76 - 058314	67 - 567303
11 - 022460	40 - 043707	78 - 785381	31 - 504482
12 - 123583	59 - 594044	44 - 315831	73 - 728088
90 - 918752	29 - 531059	53 - 260426	54 - 936954
48 - 702096	55 - 246066	96 - 050112	1 - 001123
60 - 165167	15 - 426842	17 - 652808	80 - 198757
9 - 919099	79 - 788640	20 - 092134	8 - 371897
41 - 255055	65 - 247189	23 - 235831	18 - 872910
99 - 892123	26 - 538190	77 - 732572	28 - 373036
39 - 840268	88 - 279651	38 - 774156	7 - 561785
42 - 156178	22 - 113471	72 - 187976	27 - 863921
4 - 814594	46 - 525055	57 - 762808	63 - 297961
16 - 527965	83 - 129101	51 - 866280	61 - 607741
84 - 390213	47 - 751367	66 - 257291	43 - 215372
37 - 654044	19 - 826022	85 - 433257	32 - 714594
86 - 094370	14 - 225729	92 - 601123	10 – 921011
6 - 251673	70 - 437077	71 - 058864	99 - 802212

How am I able to do this? Just using the method I have just introduced you to. It is simply a matter of attacking each number one by one.

Take the combo **30 – 420121** for example.

There are three simply steps:

1. Convert each number to its phonetic equivalent

3   0   -   4   2   0   1   2   1

M S - R N S D N T

2. Create words by adding vowels

MouSe   -   RuNS DowN iT

3. See the visual association in your mind's eye

I think of the old nursery rhyme, "Tick tock, the mouse ran up the clock..." Well I guess the mouse also runs down it too!

Lets do the second one, **69 – 314781**.

6   9   -   3   1   4   7   8   1
SH P   - M T R K F T
SHiP   - MoTheR CraFT

Legal Citations

One of the first jobs I had as a young man, before I began my university career, was with a police force. At that time, and I believe it is still the case, we were required to memorize a large number of sections in the criminal code.

You can imagine that this was rather arduous without any training in memory.

Today this would be a rather easy task with the use of acrostics. For example let's attack the following list. Why do I suggest the acrostic here rather than the continuation of the technique we have applied above?

The reason is that it is sometime difficult to find one word that describes or, is readily associated with, the item we wish to recall.

For example there are only so many words in the English language that contain the consonant sounds three, three and six. The section of the criminal code dealing with indecent or harassing telephone calls. It would take a good deal of time to find them and they may not be very descriptive.

If, on the other hand, we use an acrostic, we open up the entire dictionary because, as you will recall, it is only the first letter in a word that has meaning or acts to represent a number.

Consider the following list:

Section	Offence
336	Indecent Telephone Calls
307	Counterfeiting
254	Bigamy

119	Personating a Police Officer
247	Kidnapping
87	Carrying a Concealed Weapon
244	Assault
389	Arson
338	Fraud
120	Perjury

In dealing with the first offence, indecent or harassing telephone calls – 336, we will first decode the section into its phonetic equivalent and then choose three words that we can associate with the actual offence. For example:

1. Indecent Telephone Calls

3   3   6

M   M   Sh

My Mother Shocked

A few more examples are shown below:

2. Counterfeiting

3   0   7

M   S   K

Making Sawbucks Criminal

----

3. Bigamy

2   5   4

N   L   R

Numerous Lovers Restricted

----

4. Personating a Police Office

1   1   9

D   D   P

Don't Dress Police-like

5. Kidnapping

2	4	7
N	R	K
Never	Release	Kidnappers

----

6. Carrying a Concealed Weapon

8	7
F	C
Firearm	Concealed

----

7. Common Assault

2	4	4
N	R	R
Knuckle	Remedy	Restricted

8. Arson

3	8	9
M	F	B
Make	Fires	Burn

----

9. Fraud

3	3	8
M	M	F
Make	Money	Fast

----

10. Perjury

1	2	0
T	N	S
Tell	No	Stories

Dates and Appointments

Another system I'd like to introduce you to is the system remembering dates and appointments.

While the principle behind the system is essentially the same as other numbers, there are a couple of refinements that improve its effectiveness.

What we need to do is come up with something that will give personality to both the days in the month and the months in the year.

We could, of course, use the peg system to represent both the days of the month and the months of the year, but this might lead to confusion since we'd be using the same peg for the days of the month and the months of the year. It is better to create separate words or pegs for each of the months in the year and use our established peg words *solely* for the days in the month.

The choice of these "Month Pegs" is very intuitive and for that reason take virtually no time to learn.

Since January finds us in the coldest, snowiest day of the year we might choose SNOWMAN. February, because of Saint Valentine's Day might suggest a HEART, March LEPRECHAUN, because St. Patrick's Day falls in that month.

April SHOWERS bring May FLOWERS, takes care of those two months and we will choose BRIDE for June because it is typically the month most people still choose to marry. FIRECRACKER for July because of Independence Day and Canada Day. August finds us in the middle of the summer when many people vacation on some BEACH. September is when

SCHOOL starts and a PUMPKIN symbolizes the scary month of October, Thanksgiving in November suggests a TURKEY (Canadians might select a SOLDIER for Remembrance Day), and Christmas in December suggests SANTA CLAUS. So we have the following list of month pegs:

The Month Pegs

January	Snowman
February	Heart
March	Leprechaun
April	Showers
May	Flowers
June	Bride
July	Firecracker
August	Beach
September	School
October	Pumpkin
November	Turkey
December	Santa Claus

How might this system be applied to remember birthdays or anniversaries or an important meeting or the day and month of any event in history?

Let's say you wished to remember the following five events:

Your Assistant's Birthday	**May 1st**
Visit Special Friend in San Francisco	**February 13th**
Your Vacation Begins	**August 18th**
Company Picnic	**June 9th**
Speak to Lions Club	**November 16th**

You wanted to remember that your assistant's birthday is May 1st. We have committed to our memory the Month Pegs and therefore will use the peg "flowers" to represent the month of May. Using our normal peg system we will use "tie" to represent the day of the month.

Now all that is left is again to form a distinctive visual image joining these two with your assistant. Why not see yourself handing your assistant a big bouquet of flowers, tied together with a man's necktie. Take a moment to see this image in your mind's eye.

Secondly we don't want to forget that we will be flying to San Francisco on February 13th to see that *special* someone.

Using the same technique you will select "heart" for the month peg and "time" for the day in the month. Here I might want to remember that it is time to leave my heart in San Francisco again.

Thirdly, I wish to recall that my vacation begins August 18th.

I would see myself dug into the sand on the beach watching a tiny TV. I am so addicted to Oprah that I spend my vacation time watching her; see yourself in this absurd situation before we go on.

The company picnic is June 9th this year.

See you and your colleagues sitting around a picnic table as a wild eyed bride, still dressed in her wedding gown, runs through the picnic ground chased by a swarm of Texas killer bees.

And finally, you need to be sure not to forget that you will be speaking at the Lions Club on November 16th.

Well you know that your month peg for November is "turkey" and your regular peg for 16 is dish. Why not see a lion eating a huge turkey out of a serving dish.

Can this system be applied to remember the day and month that historical events took place?

Certainly, let's try a few. Please be sure to see each of the following descriptions in your mind's eye:

1.   **First lunar landing**   July 21st
2.   **President Obama's Birthday**   August 4th
3.   **Lady Gaga's Birthday**   March 28th

The first lunar landing was July 21st. See that cutup, that "nut" Neil Armstrong stepping onto the moon and the first thing he does is lights and throws a firecracker. See the puff of moon dust.

President Obama is so stressed from the demands of the presidency that he spends his vacation with a bottle of rye dug into the sand at the beach.

Lady Gaga on the other hand celebrates her birthday by knifing a leprechaun.

We can do more or less the same thing to recall weekly events. Again to avoid confusion, we must create seven *new* pegs to represent the days of the week.

I have created the following day pegs:

The Day Pegs

Sunday	**Church**
Monday	**Hammer**
Tuesday	**Newsday**
Wednesday	**Camel**
Thursday	**Thruway**
Friday	**Fish**
Saturday	**Latter-day**

Church is obvious for Sunday. Monday is the first workday so I chose a work tool – hammer. Newsday rhymes with Tuesday and nothing else does, we can see a busy newsroom. I actually see a CNN set with Wolf Blitzer holding a script. Wednesday, hump day suggests a camel. Thursday rhymes with thruway, a term used in the Eastern states to denote a freeway. Friday is the day Christian's (at least used to) eat fish. Saturday rhymes with latter-day. I picture two young Mormon missionaries with white shirts, ties and knapsacks.

How might these day pegs be used to help us remember upcoming events, for example the following five?

1. **The cable guy installation Monday at 10:00 am**

2. **Doctor's appointment at 3:00 pm on Wednesday**

3. **Alumni meeting Saturday at 4:00 pm**

4. **Pick up Son from airport Thursday at 5:00 pm**

5. **Haircut Tuesday at 1 pm**

As we work through this list, take a moment to see the picture I am describing clearly in your mind.

To remember that the cable guy is coming over Monday at 10:00 am, select "hammer" from my day pegs and "toes" from the regular peg system. What is the image? See the cable guy pounding your toes with his hammer. Goofy? Will you recall it? Absolutely. Take a moment to see this and each of the associations that follow in your mind.

You hope to recall that you have a doctor's appointment at 3:00 pm on Wednesday. Wednesday is "hump day," our symbol being the camel and the peg word for 3 is "ma." See your mother on a camel with your doctor.

Your alumnus meeting is Saturday at 4 O'clock. Our day peg is "latter-day" and our time peg is "rye." When you arrive at your meeting you notice the room is filled with Mormon missionaries all drinking rye whisky, right out of the bottle.

Your son is flying in on Thursday at 5:00 pm. You don't want to forget to pick him up. The day peg for Thursday is "Thruway" and our peg for 5 is "law." See yourself rushing to the airport to get him. You are late and

Lighting Your Way To Excellence

speeding. You are so late you can't stop for the police car (law) that is chasing you.

Finally, your appointment for a haircut is this Tuesday at 1 pm. Newsday and tie. Well your haircut is going to be filmed by CNN so you want to put on a new tie to look your best.

Please turn the page and test your recall.

Practice Exercise 4.1
Dates & Appointments

Enter the month and day that each of the following events will take place:

1. **Your Assistant's Birthday:** _____

2. **Visit Special Friend in San Francisco:** _____

3. **Your Vacation Begins:** _____

4. **Your Company Picnic:** _____

5. **Your speech to the Lions Club:** _____

6. **President Obama's Birthday:** _____

7. **First Lunar Landing:** _____

8. **Lady Gaga's Birthday:** _____

Practice Exercise 4.2
Weekly Appointments

Enter the day and time that each of the following events will take place:

1. **Your cable installation:** _____

2. **Your doctor's appointment:** _____

3. **Your alumni meeting:** _____

4. **Pick up Son from airport:** _____

5. **Your haircut appointment:** _____

In chapter four we will introduce a second dimension to the peg concept when we discuss spatial memorization.

Chapter Five

Spatial Memorization

Sometimes it's necessary for us to remember where things fall spatially. Because of this, I've developed something I call the memory matrix, on the next page you'll see an example of it.

In the development of the memory matrix, I've come up with a series of letter pegs to represent the letters in the alphabet A to Z, these pegs are simply animal names that begin with each of the letters in the alphabet.

A – Ape	N – Nightingale
B – Bear	O – Ostrich
C – Cow	P – Pig
D – Dog	Q – Quail
E – Elephant	R – Rabbit
F – Fox	S – Snake
G – Goat	T – Turtle
H – Horse	U – Unicorn
I – Iguana	V – Vulture
J – Jackal	W – Weasel
K – Kangaroo	X – Ox
L – Lamb	Y – Yak
M - Mouse	Z - Zebra

The reason for creating this second peg system is to allow us to describe a spatial relationship among and between items. By creating a matrix with the alphabet pegs running across the X or horizontal axis and the numbered pegs down the Y or vertical axis we are able to allocate a spatial identification allowing us to see how things relate one to another in two dimensions.

The example I have provided is the periodic table, we can locate and recall spatially in our mind, the location of any one of the elements through the unique combination of letter and number pegs. Gold, for example, is K6, to remember that, I'm going to convert K6 to its pegs – letter and number. K is kangaroo and six is shoe.

All that is left is to form a visual association between kangaroo, shoe and gold. The image would choose is of a kangaroo jumping around in golden shoes.

The Periodic Chart

	A	B	C	D	E	F	G	H	I	J	K	L	M	N	O	P	Q	R
1	H																	He
2	Li	Be											B	C	N	O	F	Ne
3	Na	Mg											Al	Si	P	S	Cl	Ar
4	K	Ca	Sc	Ti	V	Cr	Mn	Fe	Co	Ni	Cu	Zn	Ga	Ge	As	Se	Br	Kr
5	Rb	Sr	Y	Zr	Nb	Mo	Tc	Ru	Rh	Pd	Ag	Cd	In	Sn	Sb	Te	I	Xe
6	Cs	Ba	Lu	Hf	Ta	W	Re	Os	Ir	Pt	Au	Hg	Tl	Pb	Bi	Po	At	Rn
7	Fr	Ra	Lr	Rf	Db	Sg	Bh	Hs	Mt	Uun	Uuu	Uub		Uuq				
8																		
9			La	Ce	Pr	Nd	Pm	Sm	Eu	Gd	Tb	Dy	Ho	Er	Tm	Yb		
10			Ac	Th	Pa	U	Np	Pu	Am	Cm	Bk	Cf	Es	Fm	Md	No		

If I wanted to remember that arsenic in our chart was O4, well, I would come up with my animal peg for the Letter O, which is ostrich, our regular peg for four, which is "rye." Arsenic is located at O4 I would again convert O4 to its number and letter pegs – "ostrich" and "rye" and then visually associate it with arsenic. I may see the poor ostrich dropping dead after it drank some rye whisky laced with arsenic.

The Periodic Chart

The memory matrix is particularly useful for applications in geography and mapping.

If, for example, you are visiting a new and strange land or city for the first time, by taking a few minutes in advance to superimpose you memory matrix on the landscape you will have a pretty good lay of the land before you step foot on it.

For example, let's assume that I am planning to visit Washington, D.C. for the first time and you don't want to be seen as the typical tourist folding and unfolding maps continuously, I have instead decided to apply my memory matrix.

Below is a map of Washington, D.C. with the memory matrix superimposed:

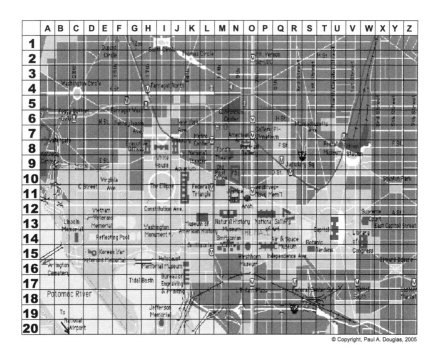

Let's say that my hotel is located at H1, well, using our letter pegs, we know that H stands for "horse," and of course our peg word for one is "tie." I might picture myself tying up my horse to the hitching post just outside my hotel!

My Hotel

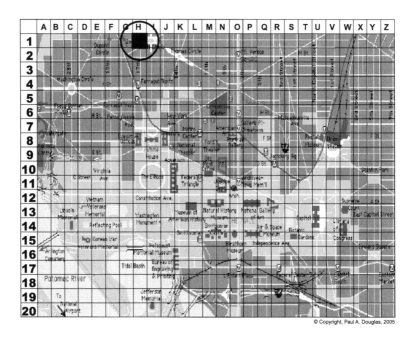

© Copyright, Paul A. Douglas, 2005

I might picture in my mind's eye the image of tying my horse up outside my hotel.

The White House

Now, one of the attractions I hope to visit that day is the White House, which on our matrix map is at cell "I9." We know that our animal peg for I is "Iguana," and our peg for nine is bee, I might see Barack Obama, the current resident of the White House, riding an iguana on the West lawn and being chased by George Bush's pet Texas killer bees:

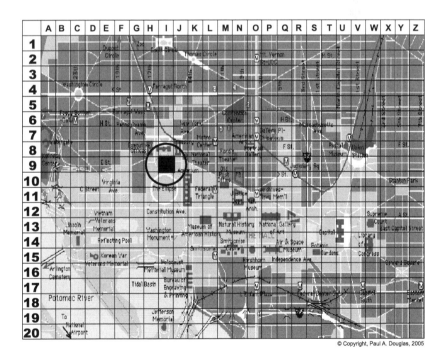

Another place I hope to see that day is the Smithsonian; looking at my matrix I can see that it is located at K15. K is kangaroo and fifteen is tail. I would see a Godzilla-sized kangaroo sitting in front of the Smithsonian with its enormous tail wrapped around the building.

The Smithsonian Museum

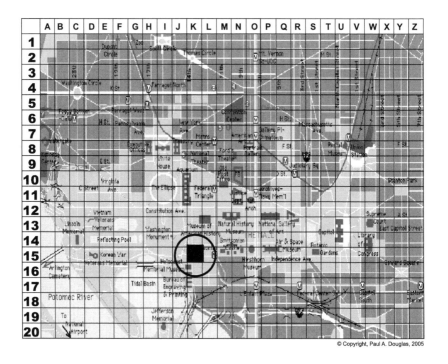

The capital building is located at T13. Turtle and time. The Capital Building has a huge dome and rotunda. It would take that poor, determined turtle days to circle it.

The Capital Building

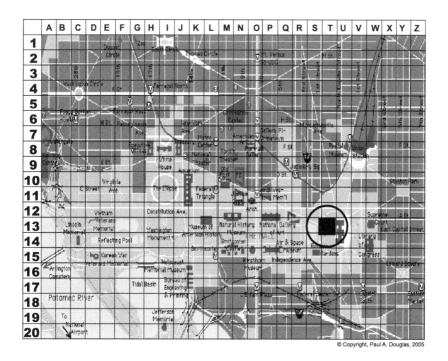

OK, now let's say I am located at the Lincoln Memorial, which is at C14 and want to walk back to my hotel (long walk), which way would I head?

Well I recall tying up my horse outside my hotel (H1), so my hotel is a little bit East and a long way North.

Getting to My Hotel

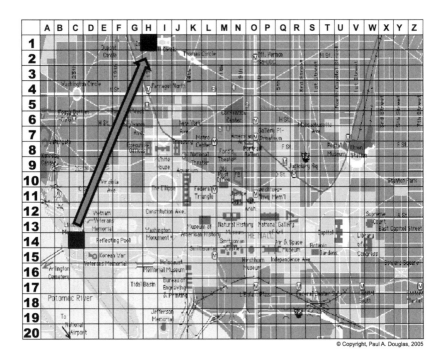

If I wanted to walk from the Capital Building to the White House, which direction should I head?

Well I know I am at location T13 (That poor turtle is still trying to circumnavigate the rotunda) and that the White House is at location I9 (Obama on iguana being chased by bees). So this tells me I need to walk West and North.

Capital Building to White House

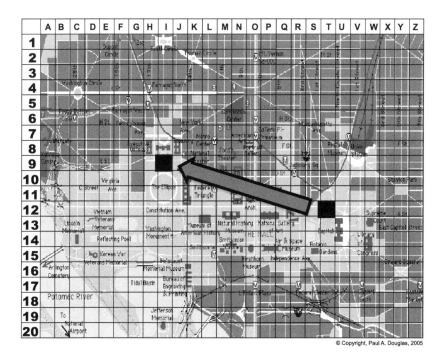

© Copyright, Paul A. Douglas, 2005

There is another variation on this matrix that might work better in some applications. This is where we give an individual personality to each cell within the matrix by giving it a unique peg identity. Let's call them Matrix Pegs.

All cells in **Column A** will be represented by peg words that begin with the letter "A." All cells in **Column B** will begin with the letter "B." All cells in **Column C** will start with the letter "C," and so on.

The second sound in the Matrix peg will be the phonetic sound for the row number.

For example the matrix pegs for the first column would be A1 – Auto, A2 – Annie, A3 – Ammo, A4 – Arrow, A5 – Ale, A6 – Ash, A7 – Aqua, A8 – AV, A9 – Ape and A10 – Aussie. The second column would be B1 – Bat, B2 – Ben, B3 – Beam, B4 – Bear, etc. Column C, C1 – Cat, C2 – Can, C3 – Comb and so on.

You will note that in this system the number 10 takes on the phonetic sound for zero. This underscores the limitation of this approach. You are limited to ten rows and 26 columns for a total of 260 cells; in the first approach, using animal peg /regular peg combinations there is no limit to the number of rows we could use.

Let's return our attention to the periodic chart; to remember the position of gold I would associate it with the Matrix Peg for K6 which is "cash." To remember that A1 is the location of hydrogen, I would associate it with "auto," my matrix peg for A1. I might see all the automobiles in the future running on hydrogen. To remember that iron is H4, I would associate it with "hair" the matrix peg for that location.

Chapter Six
Public Speaking

According to the Book of Lists, glossophobia, the fear of public speaking ranks first as the greatest fear most people have. When asked to list their top ten fears the majority of people put speaking in public higher up their list than their fear of death! Fear of dying was a lowly seventh on the list with fear of heights (acrophobia) being number two and fear of spiders (arachnophobia) being number three.

I heard a witty comment that most people would rather be in the coffin than delivering the eulogy.

It is a common fear, it happens to the most intelligent and creative of us. The great Mark Twain had a debilitating fear of speaking in public. Once, when asked to give an impromptu speech on leadership, he was so gripped with fear that he stood up and said, "Caesar and Hannibal are dead, Wellington has goon to a better place, Napoleon is under the sod and to be honest I don't feel too good myself."

I once had a great fear of public speaking. In my religion, young people are asked, forced really, from an early age to speak from the podium in church. I can remember as a boy of twelve or thirteen sitting at the front of the congregation with my knees literally shaking, as I waited for my turn to step up to the podium.

Now I speak on a regular basis to groups of from one or two hundred to several thousand and I do it without written notes. If you are supposedly some big memory expert, stepping up to the mike with a handful of notes wouldn't cut it. I'd be laughed out of the room.

I have overcome my fear of public speaking by overcoming my fear of forgetting what I wanted to say. You see most people are not fearful of speaking in public because they don't have anything to say, it is because they fear they will lose their place of draw a blank when they look out at that sea of faces showing pity and embarrassment for us.

I personally believe that the best public speakers were not born with that gift but rather they learned to be good at it. They developed a method or system that worked so well for them that their fears simply evaporated.

But make no mistake here your fear of speaking in public can have a very negative impact on your business and professional life. As we advance in our organizations and careers the one thing we can count on is that we are increasingly going to be required to give presentations and speeches. Your inability to confidently deliver a talk or speech means lost opportunities.

If you allow your nervousness to get the best of you, it can *and will* affect your credibility and the level of professionalism you exude.

But why is it such a significant fear? What is at the root? Why do we angst so much about doing something we have done since our first year of life – speaking?

Unquestionably one of the reasons so many people dread speaking in public is the fear of ridicule. We perceive that the people in the group, whatever the size of the group, be it 5, 50 or 500, will be critically judging us and as a result our self-image our self-esteem will be eroded.

But when you examine this fear, for most people it really comes down to a worry about forgetting, specifically, forgetting what to say next.

Many people overcome this perceived risk of forgetting by essentially reading their speeches, either from a stack of papers or index cards.

But the rapport with your audience is built with the eyes, not the voice, and if your head is bobbing up and down constantly the effect is less than inspiring. There is a perceivable gap as your eyes go from the long gaze to the audience to the short focus on your notes. As well, there is still a danger of losing your place in the text and God help you if you drop your stack of cards on your way to the podium.

Eye contact is the key to good delivery, and anything that detracts from that weakens your speaking ability, using index cards still requires that you remove your eyes from the audience while you scan them. It can also ruin a high point when you have to use fillers such as *er, um, uh* as you scan the card.

The first thing you need to do is believe in your knowledge and ability – to believe in yourself. If you didn't know anything, people wouldn't be asking you to speak. You have the knowledge and wisdom, and people really want to hear what you have to say.

The second most important thing is preparation. The more you prepare, the more confident you will be.

The problem is most people, even accomplished successful executives and professionals, don't know how to prepare properly.

An enormous amount of time, often a week's work or more, will go into a one-hour speech, writing and rewriting the speech so it can be memorized word for word.

Perhaps this allotment of time and all the stress associated with it could be justified if the result was spectacular, but too often it results in a stilted presentation and often a bored audience who senses that what they are hearing has in fact been memorized.

The good news is that, as any accomplished speaker knows, it is not necessary nor is it advisable to memorize a speech word for word.

A speech is basically a sequence of thoughts, not a sequence of words, it's not necessary nor is it wise to try to memorize your speech word for word. The most effective way to deliver a speech is to speak from thought to thought wrapping each thought in the words that come to you in that moment. If you memorize each word it will sound canned, and the pressure that comes from feeling that you must deliver it verbatim will reduce your effectiveness.

You want your speech to appear planned, not canned.

Again, if you're being asked to speak on a subject, you must have some familiarity with it. The problem most people have is not that they don't know what to say but rather that they have difficulty remembering the order of the thoughts they wish to express, the fear, then, is more one of losing your place.

The link method is ideally suited to speech preparation; after all, speech is a particular series of thoughts being expressed in a particular order. There are three steps to using the link method for speech preparation. First, you write down everything you hope to say, yes *actually write it out*. This is important as it allows you to rearrange your thoughts in a logical sequence and identify redundancies, etc. Secondly, once you are satisfied with the speech as it is written, you will then identify each of the major speaking points within it. These are the major topics you wish to express. You will then select an image that will represent visually each of the major talking points or topics in your speech. This image is an important cue, a mental picture that will remind you of the entire talking point. As you will see in what follows, this is not a particularly difficult thing to do. And finally, you will associate the visual images with a peg or loci using one of the mnemonic filing systems you have already been introduced to in this book.

Let's take the example of a CEO who has been asked to speak to the senior staff at the annual meeting for his firm. As this is one of only a few opportunities for this executive to speak to all the senior staff as a group he wants to cover as much ground as possible.

After some editing and rewriting, he has come up with the following draft for his speech:

Speech to Universal Widget

Good morning. It is a pleasure to meet with you today in Las Vegas; it's good to see so many friendly faces, some that I have known for many years and some that I have just seen for the first time today.

I am sure that many of you feel, like I do, that it is a shame that we can only get together as a large group once each year. It seems to me that the work that we do here and the relationships that we establish are very important.

I enjoyed this morning's presentation and Bob's remarks at lunch today.

I am amazed that such a young person, just out of college, could have already developed such a wealth of knowledge on this industry and its history.

I'm not sure that you know this, but when Bob was at college, he was the regional champion for College Jeopardy. In fact, but for missing one question, he would have gone on to win the national championship.

The question was, "What was George Bush's three toughest years? The correct answer, of course, was "The third grade!"

I want to thank Mary for the outstanding work she has done in getting us all here and making us so comfortable. I am sure that you will agree that her choice in venue was right on, and her attention to detail as well. The little extras she has provided have made this year's annual meeting one of the best we have ever had, thank you Mary.

I would also like to thank each and every one of you for your creativity and your dedication and the hard work that you have put into your jobs and assignments in the past year. I don't think there is another company in our industry that has developed the level of synergy that we have at Universal Widgets, and I hope that you will take this expression of my appreciation to your teams back home.

Operationally speaking, we are doing well and, with a few exceptions, we have realized the growth we hoped for. Our auditors, in their presentation last night, gave you everything you ever wanted to know about each division and I will not reiterate their summaries here. I would like, however, to draw a few conclusions.

Sales in the core products have not grown significantly, but we are holding our market share. The lack of growth in this area was partly the result of geopolitical events beyond our control and a general weakening of consumer spending, particularly in the South. On the other hand, our entertainment division has done very well as has our sporting division.

Our operations are moving into new, previously untried areas, and our traditional products and markets are being expanded. Sales are up 22% and before tax profits are up by more than 10% as well. Our overseas operations have seen incredible growth in the last year, particularly in the last two quarters. Sales in Hong Kong alone have increased by 43% and we are predicting that the growth in this emerging market will continue at the same pace for at least another three quarters.

We had our share of challenges this year. In our first quarter, as a result of legislative action, we were barred from exporting to Iraq, Iran and much of the Arab world. This was particularly difficult for our export division in that we were given less than three weeks notice of the Government's intent in this regard. Fortunately, through the effort of Jack Lane and his staff in export and our lobbyists, we were able to satisfy our political masters that the products we export are altogether non-strategic, and if anything they help to serve the humanitarian needs of these States. This bump, however, had a substantial impact on our first quarter's sales.

As well, mid-year, out of the blue, our entertainment division was hit with a lawsuit claiming copyright infringement. Totally unfounded, this frivolous claim nonetheless distracted many of us at headquarters because of the negative press we received. I am happy to report that the court of first instance, throughout this suit and our legal department, is examining the possibility of bringing an action for defamation against our detractors.

I believe, however, ladies and gentlemen, that if we are to continue to grow in the decade to come we must continue to seek new markets, products and profit centers. This is particularly important as the population here in North America ages. It has been predicted that this demographic shift will account for a 30% – 40% decrease in demand for our traditional products over the next five to eight years.

To fuel this expansion, I would like to announce today that the Board has authorized the creation of a new division for overseas operations. Located in Hong Kong, this new division will be headed by Jeff Wong, who as you know, is presently the manager of product development. Jeff will become the first Vice-President of Overseas Operations.

If you can support Jeff in this new role, please join me with your applause. Thank you, Jeff, for accepting this challenging and pivotal position.

Make no mistake, we are in a very competitive marketplace. We need to be vigilant. Our competitors are at the gate. The market itself is changing and we must work hard - each and every one of us, if we are to sustain our growth.

This is a call to arms. What we do together in the next twelve months will determine, I believe, the future of this organization. If we are to grow into a truly multinational company, then now is the time for effort. Now is the time for sacrifice. Now is the time to enhance our brand image and our customer service.

We need to continually be adding to our team. We need talented individuals who can catch our vision and possess the skills we need at this important time in our history. I want to ask each one of you as managers and executives in this company to always be on the lookout for individuals who can bring to the table those ideas and approaches that have brought this firm to where it is today. We are looking for a few good men and women who can move us forward; people who realize that it is the service that we give to our customers that will ultimately determine our collective futures.

I am of the opinion that there is no more important function that we can be involved in than customer service. It is vital. While we can certainly affect short-term profits by introducing mass produced, well marketed products; I believe that without excellent customer service, we will ultimately fail. Remember our mission statement, Quality Products and Outstanding Service.

Each one of you is an ambassador for Universal Widgets - don't forget that!

Our research has shown that we must innovate. If we stand still we are really moving backward. We need good ideas, better ideas. Be always thinking of that better mousetrap.

In this regard I am announcing the "Beemer A Quarter" incentive program, where the employee coming up with the best, most profitable idea each quarter will receive a new BMW. This program is also open to each of you. Sell it to your staff; let them understand the importance of innovation to our future.

So to conclude, my dear friends, know that we appreciate everything you do. May you continue your outstanding efforts in the coming year. We are a family here at UW. Let us strengthen and expand our family in the next twelve months. Thank you again for your efforts and your dedication. It is a great pleasure for me to lead you at this time.

Best wishes for the future.

Now remember the four steps in preparation:

Preparing a Speech

1. **Write out the speech, edit, revise and polish**

2. **Identify the major talking points in your speech**

3. **Choose a visual image and reminder for each of these points**

4. **Associate each of these images with a peg or loci**

Step One: If I were the one who would be delivering this speech I would begin by jotting down the main talking points or topics that I wanted to cover. I might then rearrange these main topics so there is coherence to what I am going to say.

I would then expand on this basic skeleton by jotting down points I wished to say under each main topic area and having done that I might rearrange and edit these sub points.

Now I am ready to flesh it out. Referring to the expanded skeleton I have created for my speech I am going to write it out just as I would like it to be delivered, word for word.

When I have arrived at a finished product, I am going to read it aloud to see how it feels and to establish the approximate running time for the speech.

Step Two: Now that I have my speech as I would *like* it to be delivered. I am going to read through it once again, this time clearly identifying the major talking points. Then I will rehearse and test whether I can speak to each of the sub-points within each speaking point. I will make a note on any I seem to miss for future reference. Often at this stage I will revise further.

Incidentally, if time permits, I would not perform step one and step two at the same time or on the same day. It is best to come at an important speech a few different times with different energies.

Step Three: Now having identified my major speaking points, I will create a visual image to represent each of these points.

Step Four: Finally in step four, I associate my visual images with a loci or peg. I might use the Body File or the Room Loci method or the regular peg system, although I personally save the peg system for other things.

Let's practice this approach on the sample Universal Widget speech above. Please note that this is a very short speech to cover all the speaking points the speaker wishes to cover. I made this speech purposely short so we might illustrate each of the elements without devoting the actual time it might take to prepare a 40 or 50-minute speech.

Universal Widgets

Step One: Write, Edit and Polish the Speech

We have done so above.

Step Two: Identifying the Major Talking Points

The first thing the speaker says in his introduction is that it is good to be here (cliché), unfortunate only do it once a year and tells a joke about Bob.

Next, he thanks Mary for all her efforts to make the meeting a success and the rest of the staff for their efforts.

Thirdly, he speaks to the current status of operations.

Next, he talks about the challenges the company has had this year.

The fifth talking point speaks about growth.

The next comments the speaker makes are regarding the fact that each employee needs to work hard if the company is to succeed.

The seventh area of discussion involves locating and acquiring new and talented people.

Next he talks about the vital need for superior customer service.

The ninth point is a call for a reawakening of innovation and the realization of its importance to continued viability.

And finally, the conclusion, wherein he recaps the most important elements of his speech.

Having identified the essential elements in the speech, growth, customer service, innovation etc., we want to be sure that if we are presented with one of these speaking points, we can deliver the detail of that topic or subject. For example under challenges, we need to speak to the fact that there was an export problem created by the government, how and by whom it was solved, as well as the entertainment lawsuit.

Step Three:

Now that we have identified ten major speaking points we want to conceive vivid mental images for each. These pictures will be a visual representation of the talking point.

In the introduction, he speaks laments how seldom they all meet and tells a George Bush joke pointed at Bob. I might see the rare assembly of Bob, George Bush and the senior staff.

The second thing he wants to do is thank Mary and the staff. I might visualize this as bowing before them as a token of your gratitude.

Third he talks about the operations of the company, a scalpel is readily associated with operations.

The fourth speaking point involves failures and challenges and other *bummers*, as a "surfer dude" would put it. I would choose that image: bum.

In number five, he talks to growth and the role of innovation in securing a better future for this organization, I would just see something growing like a cancer beyond control. Cancer is my image.

The sixth talking point is the call for hard work and effort. I might visualize myself involved in some great physical labor, sweating and enervated.

Seven is the need to attract new talent. I might visualize this as grabbing people off the street.

The eighth talking point is the importance of customer service. You want to talk about the fact that customer service is the key, that in the next twelve months if we're going to realize the same type of growth that we've experienced in the previous twelve months, our customer service has to be improved, we have to maintain all of the customers that we have as well as broaden our customer base. I might see an unhappy, red-faced customer screaming at me.

Number nine is the requirement of thought and innovation. I might picture the famous statue The Thinker by French sculptor Auguste Rodin.

And finally, he capsulates and concludes with thanks, I would visualize a man's cap.

We now have ten mental images that will cue me in to the ten major talking points in my speech. To test my readiness, I may write a description of each of these images on an index card and see if looking at the card I can then deliver each element and detail I hoped to for each talking point.

Step Four: Associate You Images with A Loci or Peg

Here we have many options; we could associate each of our images with a feature of the room we will be speaking in or use something like the Body File system to assist us.

In this example I will use the Body File system.

If you recall, the body file system identifies ten places on the body starting with our toes and moving up to our scalp.

THE BODY FILE

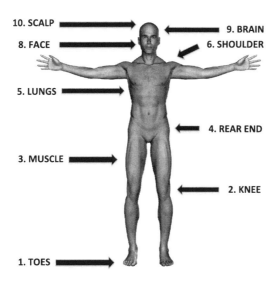

I will then begin by associating my first visual talking point image with toes. We said this image was of the rare occurrence of Bob, George Bush and the senior staff all crowded into one place, so crowded in fact, that they are standing on my toes. That is the final image I want to see in my mind. And for the purposes of this exercise, please see that in your mind's eye.

Moving up our body file, the second body part is our knees. If you recall our image of bowing and giving thanks we can alter it so that now we are doing it on our knees, like we are offering a prayer of thanks.

The large muscle in our thigh is number three and scalpel was our image. See yourself jabbing this razor sharp scalpel into this large muscle.

Our fourth body location is your rear end or your bum. Remember bummer man!

Number five is lungs and we saw an image of a cancer growing. Well we know now it is lung cancer. See a cancer growing on a lung from the size of a speck of sand to the size of a softball.

Our sixth body part is our shoulder. Why not see yourself sweating now as you put your shoulder to the wheel. Perhaps you are trying to push a wagon out of the mud.

Number seven is the collar. Our image was pulling people off the street, well now we are actually collaring them. See yourself grabbing people by the neck and dragging them into your office.

Number eight is the face. We said our image of customer service was a distraught customer screaming at you. Well now see them face to face with you, nose to nose shouting at you.

The ninth body part is brain. Certainly Rodin's Thinker was using his brain. That will work; it will help me recall the role of innovation and securing a better future for this organization.

And finally, number ten is scalp. What do you put on your scalp? A cap.

This is a wonderful way to gain greater confidence as you speak publicly and it is kind of a fun way to exercise your mind.

If you took the time to form the mental associations, then see if you can deliver the essential elements of this practice speech.

From my experience, I can testify that this system works well, and with a little practice, the confidence that you'll gain by using this method rather than written material or written notes will enhance your speaking ability.

Mnemonics and the Interview

One of the most important applications of memory to the business or professional person relates to it efficacy in the interview. As a manager or as a member of the executive team you are required to conduct a number of types of interviews. While there are many different interview types including behavioral interviews, panel interviews, "tag-team" interviews and stress interviews just to mention a few, but the vast majority of the interviews you will have will be one of the following three types:

Screening Interviews

The screening interview is a tool companies use to ensure that candidates meet the minimum qualifications required to preform the job for which they have applied.

If you are asked to fulfill this gatekeeping role, you must have well-honed skills to determine whether there is anything that might disqualify the candidate. In this interview you are not attempting to determine whether the candidate is the best fit for the position; you are really only seeking to uncover gaps in their employment history, inconsistencies or anything else that would make them a bad match.

Selection Interviews

Sometimes referred to as a personal interview, "personal" here does not necessarily mean we will be asking personal questions. Indeed asking personal questions is illegal per se. Instead we will be asking the job candidate questions about him or herself; their working style and experience. We ask all these questions in the interest of ascertaining whether or not he or she would be a good fit for the position. The candidate has made it past the selection interview and now we must determine if the candidate matches the company's need, and be able to adapt to the company's culture and goals.

Disciplinary Interviews

From time to time all managers must conduct disciplinary interviews. They are not something that we look forward to. The way in which you conduct yourself in the situation is vital to your individual success as a manager as well as the organization's viability. By definition a disciplinary interview is a meeting between one or more managers and an employee and possibly a trade union representative to investigate and deal with an employee's misconduct. Disciplinary interviews are stressful for both the manager and the employee, but their ultimate goal is to create a better environment for all employees.

The difference between a successful interview and one that falls short lies in the preparation and planning. There are five areas to look at in this preparation:

1. **Gather all the facts**
2. **Examine the employee's record**
3. **Understand your company's disciplinary procedures and policies**
4. **Look at the disposition of similar cases in the past**
5. **Draw up a structure for the interview**

The principles of memory and the mnemonic techniques we have
introduced you to in this book can greatly improve your performance in
the interview.

As in the delivery of a speech, eye contact is important in the interview.
If you essentially read to the interviewee you will miss the important
behavioral clues that your questions and comments will evoke. As well,
you can encourage the interviewee to open up and elaborate or expand on
their messages with an occasional nod of the head, *uh huh*, etc. It is
difficult to do so if your head in buried in your files.

Approach interviews as you would speeches. Create a skeletal outline of
how you would like to proceed. Like a speech, you will have an
introduction, body and conclusion. You could use several of the
mnemonic systems we have discussed including the same system we used
for our speech.

Remember that the greatest mistake managers make in conducting a
disciplinary interview is that they fail to stay on message often deviating
from their company's disciplinary policies.

Be careful not to respond emotionally to anything the interviewee may say
which is sure to take you off message. General George Patton suggested we
should act as if "you've heard it all before." Also don't jump too quickly to
write something down in response to a question you have asked, This can
make it appear as if you are surprised, shocked or pleased about an answer,
which may influence their responses to future questions.

The four steps in preparing for the interview are then:

1. Create a detailed script
2. Identify your major talking points
3. Replace each talking point with a visual image and cue
4. Use one of the mnemonic tools presented to remind you of each visual cue

With a little practice, you will find it much easier and far less stressful to prepare for and conduct highly professional interviews.

When You Are the Interviewee

If we are speaking about an employment interview, it has always be good advice to learn as much as you can about the company prior to the interview so that you might prepare intelligent questions highlighting your understanding of the job.

The five most common questions asked in job interviews are:

1. **What do you know about this company?**
2. **Why do you want to work for this company?**
3. **Would you tell me about yourself?**
4. **What skills can you offer us?**
5. **Why should we hire you?**

I'd be very surprised if you were not asked question number one at the last job interview you had. That being so, do your homework. Whether you are applying for VP finance or for an entry position, you should know as much as possible about the company or business you're going to work for.

Who are the movers and shakers in the firm? Has the company been in the news lately? You want to stand out as someone who comes prepared, and has a genuine interest in the company as well as the job. The peg system can help you here. For example, if you wanted to comment on the new government contracts the firm has landed with Egypt, Panama and the Netherlands. I might associate my peg word for number one (Tie) with a substitute for Egypt. I might see a huge necktie going all the way around one of the great pyramids in Giza. My second peg (Noah) would be trying to navigate his ark through the Panama Canal and my mother is dancing in her wooden shoes.

With regard to the other common questions I will likely be asked, I would create a list of intelligent responses and in like manner use either the peg system, body file or my home or office file to form the appropriate links.

Will there be questions I could not anticipate? Probably, Will all the questions I did anticipate be asked? Probably not. But by preparing and memorizing answers to these most common questions, you will look better prepared and motivated than most of your fellow candidates. In today's competitive job market it could provide the competitive edge you need.

Chapter Seven

Remembering Names & Faces

Undoubtedly, the greatest problem that most people have in the area of memory is their inability to remember people's names, yet nothing can improve our interpersonal skills as quickly and as much as being able to remember someone's name after only a brief introduction some time later.

If there is one thing we can teach someone at a seminar or in this book that can enhance their interpersonal skills, it's just that. Remembering names. Think about it for a moment. Why is it that you have difficulty with names? How many times after just being introduced to someone have you forgotten their name, even before they walked away?

There are really two reasons why people have trouble remembering names:

1. Recognizing individual facial uniqueness

2. Remembering the name associated with the face

One obvious problem might be that you don't hear it in the first place, I don't mean, because the person didn't say it loudly and clearly, but because you were not listening. We know that generally people are more concerned with what we have to say than with what others have to say.

You have the moves down pat. You have a lifetime of meeting people. You know that you should stick your hand out in front of you and say, "how do you do." You smile, you nod you give the impression that you're hanging onto every word. But are you?

No. As that person is speaking, you are really formulating your responses, you are thinking of something witty and clever to say, like, "Oh, hi there." That's where your mind is at; you're just not listening.

We may be blaming our memory when it is a communications problem. It is not a memory problem if you didn't know it in the first place.

How many times have you said, when meeting someone for the second time, "I recognize your face, but I can't recall your name?" You have probably heard others say it a hundred times. But have you ever heard someone say, "No, no, I know what your name is; it's your face that doesn't do anything for me."

Why is it that people have more difficulty remembering names than faces, why is it, that if you and I meet briefly and then don't see one another for several weeks, we will more likely to recognize each other's face than remember each other's name?

Well, the obvious thing is that remembering the face is a visual task whereas remembering the name is largely an auditory task and you will remember from chapter two that 65% of people are visual minded. But there's much more to it than that. At the root of the problem is the absolute difference that exists between recognition and recall.

Do you remember back in school the two types of the tests that you were given? One was the direct-recall type of test. This was the "fill in the blank" type of question where we were asked something like, "What's the capital of California? But there was another type of test they gave us as well, which tested essentially the same thing but in a slightly different way. It read,

"Which of the following cities is the capital of California?" And then there would be a list - Los Angeles, San Francisco, Sacramento, San Diego, Toronto, etc.

Which did you prefer as a student, the multiple-choice test or the direct recall?

Most people will respond multiple-choice. They may not be able to remember Sacramento, but when given a list, they are more likely to recognize it as being the correct response.

This is entirely analogous to names and faces, when you meet someone for the second time, remembering the face is like being given a multiple choice test, the face, the answer is in front of you, you only have to recognize it, like you had to recognize Sacramento from the list above.

But remembering the name is a direct-recall task. You have to search through your mind and find that piece of vague and nebulous information, the individual's name and then put it to the face. And to complicate things further, you have to do it under a certain amount of pressure. When we meet someone for the second time, our subjective state is heightened. If nothing else, you might be thinking, "I hope I don't forget his name." It is in this environment and under this type of pressure that we must learn to quickly put the name to the face, and as you know, it's not always easy to do so.

In this chapter we will show you how to do so. We will present the seven-step system that will enable you to lock names to faces to the extent that if you recognize the face, you will also recall the name. What we are going to do is make both the remembering of the name as well as the face a recognition task.

The Seven Steps

1. Hear the Name

The first step is to be sure to hear the name. Now, you may think, "Well, obviously, that's common sense, you have to hear the name." It may be common sense, but it's not common practice. Many people fail to remember people's names because they don't hear them in the first place; not because the other person didn't say their name loudly and clearly but rather because they weren't listening to them.

Learn to listen for names. If you miss it, say something like, "I'm sorry, sir. I missed your name," or "I'm sorry, ma'am, could I have that again."

It's not a memory problem if you didn't know it in the first place, that is a communications problem.

2. See the Name

Even after a brief introduction, take the time to see the name in your mind's eye, in big block letters: **S-m-i-t-h, J-o-n-e-s, D-o-u-g-l-a-s,** get your sense of sight involved; it's the strongest sense that you have. All of the mnemonic systems we have discussed in this book required you to SEE pictures in your mind's eye.

I'm sure you can still remember the first list we presented in chapter two that began with tree then airplane, envelope and so on. Can you recall the rest?

You were probably still able to remember that list. Why? In part because of the associations that we created but largely because you were required to form visual mental images in you mind, you got your sense of sight involved for you see, id doesn't matter if you see something directly, or if you see it in your mind's eye, in terms of recall, it is the same thing.

Abraham Lincoln, as the story goes, used to read everything aloud. People would say to him, "Abe, can't you read silently, you're driving me crazy?" His response was always, "Yes I can, but I've found that by reading aloud, I remember more of what I'm read." Why? Because he got two senses involved; his sense of sight by seeing those words printed on the page but also his sense of hearing. We want to get your sense of sight involved. See the name.

3. Comment on the Name

"Wow, that's a stupid name."

No, not that kind of comment, but draw your attention to it. Perhaps you might ask about the derivation, ask if they're related to someone you know with the same name, or compliment the name, "That's, a pretty name, is that Ukrainian?" And they'll respond, "O'Hara, I don't think so!"

All kidding aside, if you draw your attention to the name by commenting on it, you force yourself to concentrate on it. Remember the art of memory is the art of concentration. Comment on the name, where possible.

4. Use the Name

Repetition - use the name, even in the briefest conversation, it's possible to use the other person's name a couple of times. Rather than say something like, "How do you do," or "It's nice to meet you," say, "How do you do Ms. Smith" or "It's nice to meet you Doctor Anderson."

When you ask a question, you might want to preface that question with the person's name and when you're saying goodbye, force yourself to use the name again, use the name.

These first four steps are not really part of the mnemonic. They're not part of the system, but they are important steps in effective communication.

If, from this day forward, you got in the habit of making sure you heard the name; seeing it in your mind's eye; focused your concentration by commenting on it and forcing yourself to use it, you would remember many more names than you do right now, but you would still forget some. It's the last three steps that really close the system and ensure you don't forget anyone's name.

5. Substitution

Step number five is substitution. This is a very important step. You must create a pictorial equivalent or visual representation of the name. This pictorial equivalent must be something you can see clearly in your mind's eye.

We have actually practiced doing this already to some extent when in chapter four we memorized the president's names, you may recall we said there were two ways we can do so. Firstly, we can see something more concrete in our mind's eye which has the same name. The image we saw in our mind for Washington was the Washington Monument, for Adam it was Adam & Eve, for Jefferson the Jefferson Airplane and so on. Secondly, when no concrete pictorial equivalent is available or occurs to us, we choose something phonetically close. For example, Van Buren becomes a "van of blue," Polk became "poke," Buchanan became "cannon."

There is no name that you cannot create a phonetic substitute for. With long or foreign sounding names you have to break them into syllables, but it is really not that difficult.

For example, Adamkiewicz. Unless this is your name, you will not likely find a pictorial equivalent from your experience. But what does it sound like? It sounds like "damn witch!" That is an image you can see in your mind's eye.

Consider the list below:

Cameron	**Smith**	**Donaghy**
Arnold	**Campbell**	**Lamoureux**
Gore	**Chandler**	**Foster**
Archer	**Eaton**	**Holland**
O'Hara	**Flynn**	**Beacon**
Jones	**Ginsberg**	**Boyd**
Bagnell	**Cooney**	**Chisholm**
Gill	**Phillips**	**Evans**
Wolf	**Berg**	**Forrester**
Bradley	**Riley**	**Gladstone**

Some of these names you have experience with and will find it relatively easy to create a pictorial equivalent. For others, a phonetic substitute will be required.

Cameron – You might see a famous Cameron, such as the famed director James Cameron or the actress Cameron Diaz, but if you cannot think of anything or anyone with the same name, you might choose a phonetic substitute such as "camera."

Arnold - Here you might visualize Arnold Schwarzenegger or perhaps Arnold the pig.

Gore – You might think of Al Gore or Leslie Gore or, failing that, "blood and gore,"

Archer – Perhaps this suggest an archer such as Robin Hood or an arch or maybe "Archie Bunker."

O'Hara – Scarlett O'Hara or Maureen O'Hara or O'Hare Field in Chicago.

Jones – You may see Jennifer Jones or Davy Jones or Jim Jones. A phonetic substitute might be "bones."

Please take a few minutes to work through the remainder of the list or try your hand (or should I say mind) with the following list of the most common surnames in America:

The 50 Most Common Surnames in America

1. Smith	12. Thomas	23. Lewis
2. Johnson	13. Jackson	24. Lee
3. Williams	14. White	25. Walker
4. Jones	15. Harris	26. Hall
5. Brown	16. Martin	27. Allen
6. Davis	17. Thompson	28. Young
7. Miller	18. Garcia	29. Hernandez
8. Wilson	19. Martinez	30. King
9. Moore	20. Robinson	31. Wright
10. Taylor	21. Clark	32. Lopez
11. Anders	22. Rodriguez	33. Hill

34. Scott   40. Carter   46. Campbell
35. Green   41. Mitchell   47. Parker
38. Gonzales   42. Perez   48. Evans
39. Nelson   45. Phillips   49. Edwards
36. Adams   43. Roberts   50. Collins
37. Baker   44. Turner

6. Identify a Feature

Step number six, identify a feature, is often the most challenging yet with a little practice it can become very easy, no two faces are exactly alike, and that's why this step is not really that difficult when you know how.

You must learn to really look at faces. You need to identify what it is that makes one face different from another.

Many people, however recognize that faces are different and can also remember faces well without really identifying the features that make each face different.

To be proficient in remembering names and faces it is important that you can identify what *specifically* makes one face different than another.

There are seven major facial features you can look to in establishing differences:

1.   **Facial Shape**

2.   **Eyes**

3.   **Eyebrows**

4.   **Nose**

5. Jaw and Chin

6. Lips and Mouth

7. Hair

There are a number of other features that also contribute to facial uniqueness –wrinkles, teeth, moles, warts and the color and texture of the face itself.

A good place to start is with the shape of the face. There are six basic facial shapes as the following figure shows:

The Six Facial Shapes

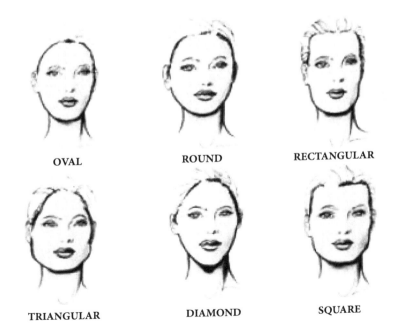

OVAL   ROUND   RECTANGULAR

TRIANGULAR   DIAMOND   SQUARE

Eyes

The eyes, their color, shape, how far apart, how deeply set they are, all of these characteristics contribute to the uniqueness of the face.

The following sketches have been created by the software police department use to help eyewitnesses to a crime produce an approximate image of what the perpetrator looked like.

Observe how changing the eyes results in a different overall look.

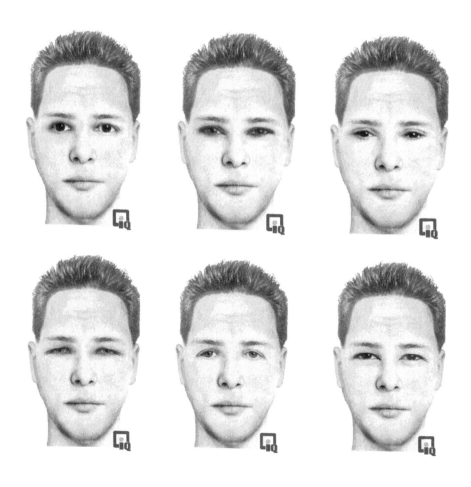

Eyebrows

The eyebrows also are important features of facial uniqueness. Compare how the difference in the eyebrows between the first and the last face results in a significant overall look.

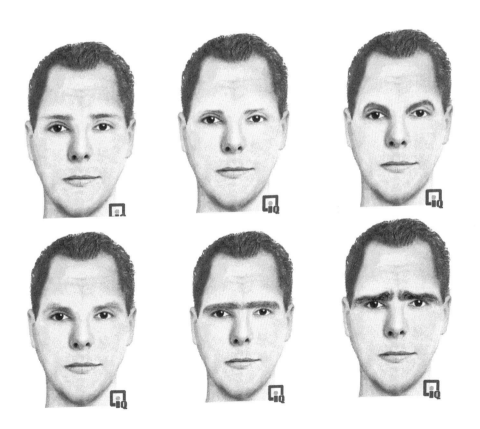

Jaw and Chin

Look at the jaw. Is it square, broad or narrow? Is the chin cleft or dimpled, pointed, double, or weak and receding?

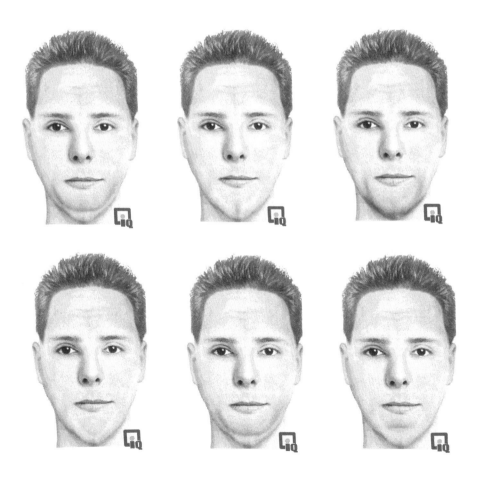

MEMORY FOR MANAGEMENT
Lighting Your Way To Excellence

The Nose

One of the most visible parts of the face is the nose. The shape of the nose is determined by the ethmoid bone and the nasal septum which mainly consist cartilage. The human nose can be found in many shapes and sizes. The human nose can be classified as being one of the following types:

Roman: This type of nose is convex in shape, like a hook.

Greek. This type of nose is perfectly straight with no curves. It is known as Greek because many Greek people have this kind of nose.

Nubian: This type of nose has wide nostrils. It is generally a little narrow at the top, broad at the middle and wide at the end. The term 'Nubian' comes from the ethnic group known as the 'Nubians' who hail from Sudan.

Hawk Nose: The hawk nose derives its name from the fact that it is convex, looking almost like a bow. Thin and sharp, it resembles the beak of a Hawk.

Snub Nose: This type of nose is as short as a nose can be and is neither sharp, wide nor hook-like.

Celestial: This type of nose is turned up and runs continuously from the eyes towards the tip

The Nose

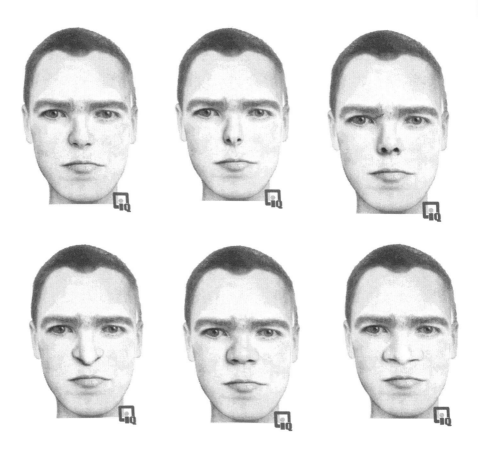

Lips and Mouth

Look at the upper lip. Is it considerably thinner than the lower lip, or are they of equal proportion? Would you describe the lips as full? Are the lips narrow or tightly pursed? Is the mouth large or small? Does the mouth turn down or is there an upward curve?

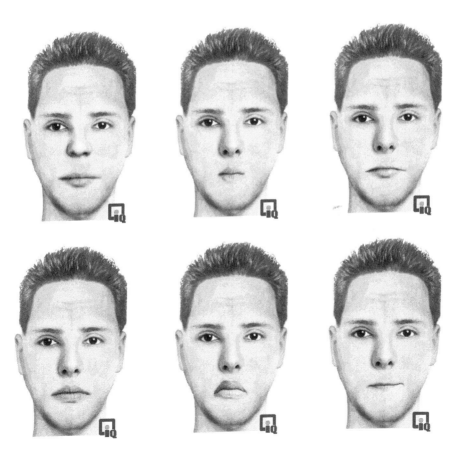

Hair

When it comes to hair, we have a lot to work with. There is color; is it blonde, brunette, redhead, black, salt and pepper or grey? There is type, is it wavy, curly or kinky? How about length? Is it long, short or, in the case of men, absent? And then of course there is the myriad of styles.

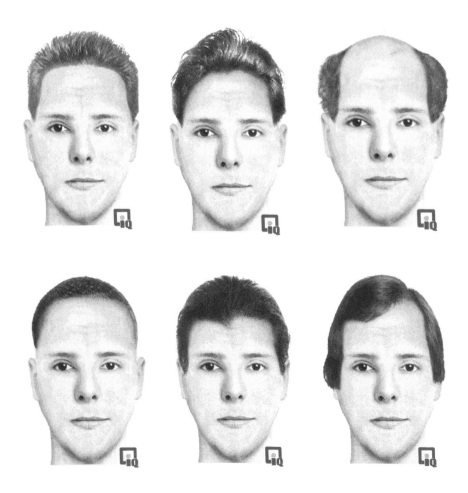

Look to all of these facial features as you attempt to identify facial uniqueness. It is essential that in step six we find *something* to which we can form an association with the substitute we created in step five.

7. Apply the "Mental Slap"

It is here in step seven where we bring the whole thing together, I call it the mental slap in part to remind you that absurd is the operative word.

In this vital step we absurdly associate the substitute we created in step five with the feature we identified in step six.

Let me give you an example of how it works, some years ago I met a man by the name of Strembitsky. At that time I had never met anyone with that name, nor had I heard it before. It was totally new to me but it was important for me to remember Dr. Strembitsky' name.

As I was being introduced to this fellow, I was thinking to myself; "What is a possible substitute for "Strembitsky?" Well, years ago I had learned to downhill ski, and at that time I was taught, as all novice skiers are, a simple turn called a Stem Christie. That popped into my mind, Stem Christie wasn't dead on, but it was close enough to remind me of Strembitsky, if when I look at this man's face, this image of Stem Christie comes out, I knew I could remember it.

Looking at this man's face, I now tried to identify a feature, maybe one that might remind me of the idea of skiing or ski jumps or Stem Christies, well, it would be nice if he had a nose like a ski jump, but he didn't. It seldom works out that way.

What he did have, however, was a fairly wide mouth, that was the feature my eye travelled to.

What did I see in my mind's eye as I attempted to form the association step seven demands?

I absurdly associated that wide mouth with my substitute, Stem Christie By seeing that wide mouth being held open by a little miniature ski. The idea being, the next time I see him, I will see that large mouth being held open by a ski, the ski will remind me of Stem Christie – Strembitsky!

You may thinking, "Wow, step seven is really four steps." No it's not; it's a process. With practice you will find that your mind will jump to this process. Remember, all you need is a cue, all you need is some short clue, and your mind will fill in the rest.

In the following few pages you will be introduced to a number of people who you, of course, have never met before.

In this exercise we will apply our seven-step model.

Our focus will be on the individual's last name only. We will discuss first names later.

We will skip over steps 1 through 4 – Hear it, see it, comment on it and use it, as these people are not really with us. These are important steps that you would always employ in the actual application of the system.

Let's turn the page and begin by meeting Ms. Phyllis Macdonald. Then turn to page xx for an illustration of how we would associate the name Macdonald with her face.

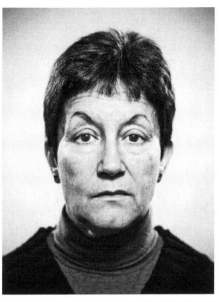

No. 1
Sheila Macdonald

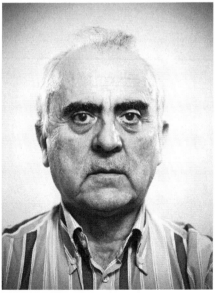

No. 2
Tom Buffett

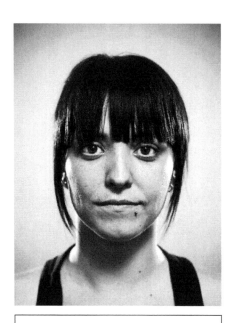

No. 3
Nancy Coyne

No. 4
Carl Oppenheimer

No. 5
Paul
Kromm

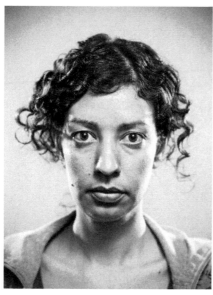

No. 6
Jan
Fowler

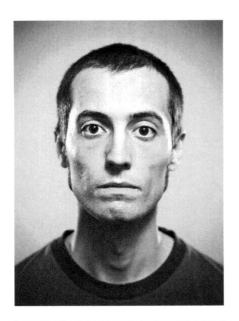

No. 7
Derek Greco

No. 8
Mary Pearson

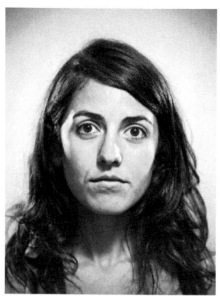

No. 9
Rosemarie Whitney

No. 10
Roger Armstrong

No. 11
John Haight

No. 12
Albert Spade

No. 13
Jeff
Stanley

No. 14
Norm
Steele

No. 15
Teddy Foreman

No. 16
Norman Small

No. 17
Nancy
Bell

No. 18
Tony
Wilson

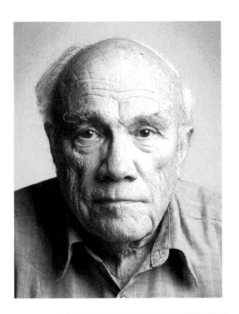

No. 19
Anderson Craig

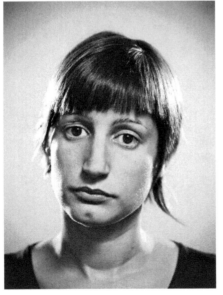

No. 20
Danielle Sharp

Sheila Macdonald

The first individual we have been introduced to is Ms. Sheila Macdonald. Again, as we meet Ms. Macdonald we will focus our attention as keenly as possible on what she says. Certainly she will tell us her name. Listen for it but if you miss it, don't let it go thinking you will pick it up in the conversation – you won't.

The second step was to see the name in your mind's eye. M-A-C-D-O-N-A-L-D, get your sense of sight involved; it is your strongest sense. Comment on her name, if possible and of course use it, "It is good to finally meet you Ms. Macdonald. We have spoken to often on the phone."

In this exercise, we will practice the last three steps and the first of these is substitution. In this fifth step, I need to find an image that could clearly represent the name Macdonald.

You might think of "Old McDonald's Farm," or perhaps someone you know with the name Macdonald but for most of us, when we hear the word Macdonald we think of the hamburger store – McDonald's.

But the image of a McDonald's restaurant is too general. We need a clear mental image that we can associate with a facial feature. You might choose the "Big Mac" or Ronald McDonald or the golden arches.

The final choice will depend to some degree on the feature we find most notable on the subjects face. In fact, while we have created a linear listing of the seven steps, in reality the application of steps five and six really occur concurrently.

As you look back at the picture of Ms. Macdonald on page xx, what feature on her face do you find to be most unique? What did your eye first travel to?

If you are not immediately struck by a particular feature, examine the face in terms of the seven major categories of facial features we discussed earlier in this chapter – facial shape, eyes, eyebrows, lips and month, jaw and chin, the nose and hair.

Keep in mind; too, that the first feature you notice is your best bet. This is also true of your substitution. The first thing you notice this time will also be the first thing you notice the next time. Use this to your benefit.

You might select the eyebrows, which are high and arches – ah, the golden arches.

In step seven I am going to absurdly associate the "golden arches" with her eyebrows. Take a moment to look once again at Ms. Macdonald while you lock in that ridiculous mental picture.

Tom Buffett

Below Ms. Macdonald we have the picture of Mr. Buffett. We need an image that would recall the word Buffett and we want to find something on Mr. Buffett's face that we could associate that substitute with. When I met Mr. Buffett, the first thing I noticed was the two deep creases that run down from the corners of his mouth, making his face look somewhat puppet like. Puppet, for me this was close enough. Look once again at Mr. Buffett forming that absurd association.

Nancy Coyne

The third person we will meet is Ms. Coyne. The substitute is easy and obvious as Coyne or coin is an actual object, how do we associate a coin with this woman's face? She has a fairly prominent mole or beauty spot on her face. Let's see that not as a beauty spot but rather as a coin stuck to her face. You try to remove it with a pair of pliers but without success. See that before we go on. A word of warning, don't think of a specific denomination – quarter, dime, nickel etc. You don't want to end up calling her "Penny."

Carl Oppenheimer

Number four is Mr. Oppenheimer. He has a nice face, but there is nothing really eye catching. It is a very clean open face. Why not go with "open?" It somewhat rhymes with "Oppen." Lock in on this suggested connection.

Paul Kromm

The sixth person we will meet is Mr. Kromm. A Kromm, a German name that rhymes with chrome. The man is bald. While a little unkind, let's go with "chrome dome."

I should comment perhaps at this point that very often the associations we form are indeed unkind even cruel. The operative word is absurd. We want you to draw on the right side of your brain. Don't let some internal sensibility keep you from choosing the most memorable association you can. Recognize it would only be cruel if we actually shared our association, which we NEVER do. It is important that you let your imagination run wild. You are not doing anyone a disfavor if you remember his or her name.

Jan Fowler

With this in mind, let's look at number seven, Ms. Fowler. What is a substitution for Fowler? Fowl or chicken comes to mind. Look at Ms. Fowler. Well her combination of the wide-set eyes and her beak–like nose make fowl a good choice. Can you see Ms. Fowler pecking for grain?

Derek Greco

Greco, a Greek name is next. Look at the features. His eyes are great. How would you form the association? How about "gecko?"

Mary Pearson

The eighth person we meet is Ms. Pearson. The verb pierce would work well here. Now is there anything on Ms. Pearson's face that would work for you?

The eyes, her hair, the heavy eyelids. We could do something with all these. I chose the sagging skin under her chin. I would see it being pierced with a knitting needle. An unpleasant picture but it will work well. Go back and witness Ms. Pearson's piercing!

Rosemarie Whitney

Our tenth victim is Ms. Whitney. A nice looking woman, with no outrageous feature jumping out at us, so we have to be creative. She doesn't resemble a famous person with that name such as Whitney Houston. What other substitutes could we come up with? Well there is whittling or whitey. I chose the word wide. Ms. Whitney has wide eyes. Let's go with that association. Please take a moment to look at Ms. Whitney's face and formulate that connection.

Roger Armstrong

In number nine we meet Mr. Armstrong a fairly tough looking guy, in fact he could be a strong-arm man.

In Mr. Armstrong's case rather than go with a specific feature, we went with an overall look. Although less common if you get a strong impression of this sort when you meet someone go with that. The fact that their face evoked such a response will ensure this will work.

Well, we have worked through the first ten together. You should have a good working knowledge of how the system works now. Please continue through the last ten forming your own association based on the features you find most distinctive or exceptional.

When you have completed the second half of this exercise, then turn to the next page and enter the last names (not the substitutes) for the twenty people you just met.

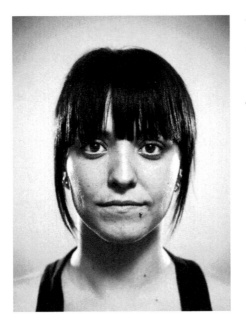

No. 1

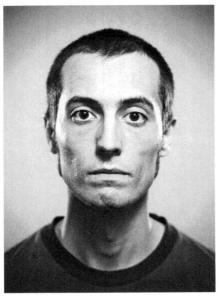

No. 2

No. 3

_____

No. 4

_____

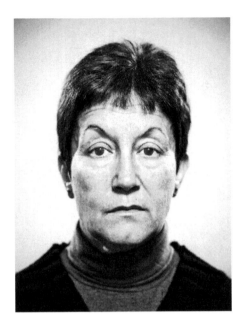

No. 5

_____

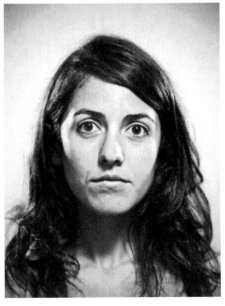

No. 6

_____

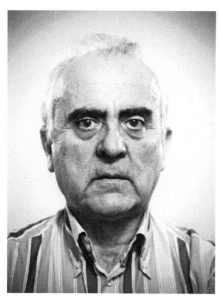

No. 7

_____

No. 8

_____

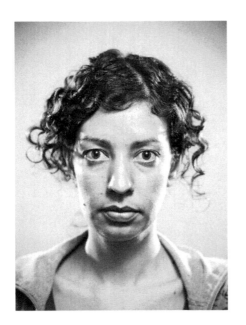

No. 9

No. 10

No. 11

_____

No. 12

_____

No. 13

_____

No. 14

_____

No. 15

_____

No. 16

_____

No. 17

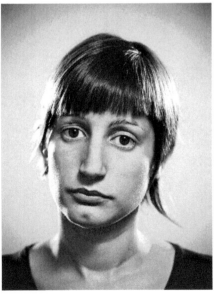

No. 18

No. 19

_____

No. 20

_____

First Names

So far our focus was on surnames but it is also important to have the ability to recall first names as well, in fact it is best to learn both.

The good news is that first names are a good deal easier than last names. The reason for this is that you will only hear between one and two hundred first names in your life, whereas you will be exposed to several thousand last names.

Because of this commonality, it follows that when you create a substitute for a first name we will use that same substitute again the next time I meet someone with that same name. In other words, when I meet a "Bill," I may choose as my substitute a dollar bill. Then with every other Bill I meet, I will use a dollar bill as my substitute. Every Mary will be the Virgin Mary; Every Joan will be Joan of Arc and so on.

Below are the most common first names in the United States:

The Most Common
Female First Names

1. Mary	9. Margaret	17. Donna
2. Patricia	10. Dorothy	18. Carol
3. Linda	11. Lisa	19. Ruth
4. Barbara	12. Nancy	20. Sharon
5. Elizabeth	13. Karen	21. Michelle
6. Jennifer	14. Betty	22. Laura
7. Maria	15. Helen	23. Sarah
8. Susan	16. Sandra	24. Kimberly

The Most Common
Male First Names

1. James	10. Thomas	19. Edward
2. John	11. Christopher	20. Brian
3. Robert	12. Daniel	21. Ronald
4. Michael	13. Paul	22. Anthony
5. William	14. Mark	23. Kevin
6. David	15. Donald	24. Jason
7. Richard	16. George	
8. Charles	17. Kenneth	
9. Joseph	18. Steven	

Let's look at the most common female names. Here are the images I use for the first column of names. Take a moment to create your own substitutes for the other two columns:

Top Female First Names

1. Mary – The Virgin Mary
2. Patricia – St. Patrick
3. Linda – Linda Ronstadt
4. Barbara – Barb (Pointed Hook)
5. Elizabeth – The Queen
6. Jennifer - Cotton Jenny
7. Maria – Marie in West Side Story (N. Wood)
8. Susan – Snoozing

Lets look at the most common Male names. Take a moment to create your own substitutes for the other two columns:

Top Male First Names

1. James – My Son
2. John – Toilet
3. Robert – Fishing Bob
4. Michael – Arch Angel
5. William – Dollar Bill
6. David – Sling Shot
7. Richard – Dick
8. Charles – Wood Chuck

Here is a tip. If you are going to a meeting with a large number of people who you will be introduced to for the first time, take the time to prepare substitutes in advance. This way when you meet someone for the first time you already have a substitute for their name. All you have to do is identify a feature and for the visual association.

A word of warning, the way to practice this system is not beginning tomorrow morning in the office with new hirers, customers, or suppliers; rather, pick up a People magazine, a Time magazine - the picture books, look at the faces of the people you don't know. Look at their names. Create your substitutes, identify their features. Lock them together.

If you'll spend just ten minutes a day reviewing random names and faces, I guarantee that you will, by the end of three weeks, become known in your organization as someone who never forgets a name.

Conclusion

As we come to the end of this book, I know that some of you probably feel somewhat overwhelmed by all the techniques and systems.

If you have read through this entire book and done each of the exercises you will see immediate improvement, but remember the mastery of these systems will take considerable practice.

Motivation in memory development, as in many other things, is paramount. Your success in developing your memory and becoming highly proficient in the systems I have presented will be proportionate to your desire or need to develop it. How much do you want to improve your memory, how much time are you willing to devote to the improvement of your memory?

The adoption of memory techniques is very much like the adoption and application of other management principles, you must *literally* change your way of behaving for long-term success. Well-established behaviors must be modified or replaced if the techniques discussed in this book are to help you in the long term.

We're living in a world of information overload, it's never been more important to know how to get the most from your memory. Start today. The next time you meet someone, apply the system for remembering names and faces. Introduce the techniques to your friends and family, teach your children. Make memory improvement and the techniques and tools presented here a part of your life.

Review this program from time to time. Be creative as you apply these techniques to fit your own particular situation.

Effort is always required, but what you will find is, with a trained memory, for the effort you expend, the results, the payoffs, will be great. I hope that this program and some of the ideas within it will lead you to greater success and perhaps even greater happiness.

I've truly enjoyed sharing these thoughts and ideas with you, I hope that they may in some way enrich your life as you develop and apply them. May I leave you with my best wishes for continued success.

Paul Douglas

Appendix A

The One Hundred Pegs

1. Tie	14. Tire
2. Noah	15. Tail
3. Ma	16. Dish
4. Rye	17. Tack
5. Law	18. T.V.
6. Shoe	19. Tub
7. Key	20. Nose
8. Ivy	21. Nut
9. Bee	22. Nun
10. Toes	23. Name
11. Tot	24. Nero
12. Tin	25. Nail
13. Time	26. Nash

27. Neck

28. Knife

29. Knob

30. Mouse

31. Mitt

32. Moon

33. Mummy

34. Mower

35. Mall

36. Amish

37. Hammock

38. Mafia

39. Mop

40. Rose

41. Rat

42. Rain

43. Ram

44. Warrior

45. Rail

46. Roach

47. Rock

48. Roof

49. Rope

50. Lassie

51. Nun

52. Lion

53. Lamb

54. Lawyer

55. Lolly

56. Leash

57. Lake

58. Leaf

59. Lip
60. Cheese
61. Shoot
62. Chain
63. Shammy
64. Sherry
65. Shell
66. Choo-choo
67. Sheik
68. Shave
69. Ship
70. Kiss
71. Kite
72. Coin
73. Comb
74. Car

75. Coal
76. Cash
77. Coke
78. Coffee
79. Cab
80. Face
81. Fat
82. Phone
83. Foam
84. Fur
85. Fly
86. Fish
87. Fog
88. Fief
89. FBI
90. Bus

91.	Bat	96.	Bush
92.	Bun	97.	Book
93.	Bomb	98.	Beef
94.	Bear	99.	Pipe
95.	Bell	100.	Thesis

Index